Helping
At-Risk Youth
— *Through* —
Physical Fitness
Programming

Thomas R. Collingwood, PhD
Fitness Intervention Technologies

Human Kinetics

Library of Congress Cataloging-in-Publication Data

Collingwood, Thomas R.
  Helping at-risk youth through physical fitness programming /
  Thomas R. Collingwood.
    p. cm.
  Includes bibliographical references and index.
  ISBN 0-88011-549-1 (alk. paper)
  1. Physical education of socially handicapped youth--United
States. I. Title.
  GV444.C65 1997
613.7'043--dc21   96-53063
                                                         CIP

ISBN: 0-88011-549-1

Developmental Editor: Patricia Sammann; **Assistant Editors:** Chad Johnson and Jacqueline Eaton Blakley; **Editorial Assistant:** Amy Carnes; **Copyeditor:** Bonnie Pettifor; **Proofreader:** Anne Meyer Byler; **Indexer:** Mary Fran Prottsman; **Graphic Designer:** Robert Reuther; **Graphic Artist:** Julie Overholt; **Cover Designer:** Jody Boles; **Illustrator:** Tim Offenstein; **Printer:** Versa Press

Printed in the United States of America   10   9   8   7   6   5   4   3   2   1

Human Kinetics
Web site: http://www.humankinetics.com/

United States: Human Kinetics
P.O. Box 5076
Champaign, IL 61825-5076
1-800-747-4457
e-mail: humank@hkusa.com

Canada: Human Kinetics
Box 24040
Windsor, ON N8Y 4Y9
1-800-465-7301 (in Canada only)
e-mail: humank@hkcanada.com

Europe: Human Kinetics
P.O. Box IW14
Leeds LS16 6TR, United Kingdom
(44) 1132 781708
e-mail: humank@hkeurope.com

Australia: Human Kinetics
57A Price Avenue
Lower Mitcham, South Australia 5062
(08) 277 1555
e-mail: humank@hkaustralia.com

New Zealand: Human Kinetics
P.O. Box 105-231, Auckland 1
(09) 523 3462
e-mail: humank@hknewz.com

Contents

Foreword

There they sat—Muhammad Ali, Joe Frazier, George Foreman, and Larry Holmes—talking with Bryant Gumbel on *Today*. Bryant asked them each this question: "Where would you be if you didn't have boxing?" Their answers were "Dead," "In prison," "On death row," and "Executed." Fortunately, the hardship, discipline, and joy of training had kept them off the streets and turned them into contenders winning at life.

These men aren't the only people who have benefited from a sport discipline. Many of us grew physically, mentally, socially, and spiritually into highly capable individuals through time spent at the Y or in other recreation programs. For more than 100 years such programs have been available to inner city kids. Young boys and girls have rubbed shoulders with healthy adults who taught them the value of self-discipline, goal setting and achieving, and good health. These youngsters have had an ideal environment for learning how to make the best effort, show compassion, and cooperate and play on a team.

In the 1970s, unfortunately, our nation walked away from these outstanding outlets that gave at-risk youth alternatives to getting in trouble. In fact, the recreation, physical education, and Y programs lost the war as sport became entertainment and business. In short, we permitted sport to build characters rather than character. This change has infuriated and disheartened many of us.

Tragically, by abandoning time-tested techniques of recreation and by abdicating power to the media, our nation has placed a host of at-risk children at the door to greater risk. As a result, America's youth face the risks of school failure, crime, drug usage, poor health, and withdrawal from society. They are also at-risk of being unproductive and underemployed citizens. Half our adolescents are at moderate risk or are extremely vulnerable. None of our youth are immune. The crisis affects all of them, regardless of economic or cultural situation.

However, there is hope in recreation and sport programs for today's youth. These programs keep youth occupied and energized in healthy, productive activities and help them improve their fitness levels. That's why I feel delighted and honored to write this foreword to Tom Collingwood's new book, *Helping At-Risk Youth Through Physical Fitness Programming*. Throughout this welcome book, you will discover hard-learned, practical advice from a man who has experienced fitness and physical training at all levels and in all venues—YMCA, sport, military, and law enforcement.

Tom shows us our power to ensure that young people, especially those at-risk, are given a variety of experiences including physical fitness, physical activity, and training to help them grow into responsible citizens. Research demonstrates that youth who have healthy, active lifestyles can cope better with stress and deal more effectively with difficult issues. Through physical training on a regular basis, young people potentially can

- improve their fitness levels,
- enhance self-esteem,
- reduce their risk of heart disease,
- reduce anxiety and depression, and
- alleviate attention-deficit and learning disorders.

Physical training

- plays a vital role in alcohol and drug treatment programs,
- provides an alternative to drug and alcohol use, and
- mitigates antisocial behaviors.

I applaud Tom Collingwood on his book and encourage every reader to heed these words. Midnight basketball is not some frill: It is a necessary component of a complex society. Like most physical activity programs, it allows young people to release their frustrations, work toward a goal, be active—rather than passive—participants in life, and experience the thrill of conquering challenges.

The discipline needed for running, push-ups, lifting weights, shooting hoops, and other physical activities produces desirable results. For at-risk youth, these experiences can mean the difference between hope and despair, love and hate, life and death. As the boxing champions revealed, physical activity can help all youth be winning contenders!

Charles T. Kuntzleman
Director, Fitness for Youth
Division of Kinesiology
University of Michigan

Preface

"Sound mind–sound body" is an old saying whose meaning has been reinforced by my personal and professional experience over and over again. I am of the "old school," having learned the value of exercise as a survival skill—first through athletics, then through experience in the military and law enforcement. My experience has proven to me that the sound mind–sound body concept is more than a saying; it is a cardinal principle of human development.

When we face the challenge of making a difference with youth, especially at-risk youth, we learn to seek all potential avenues to help our clients, students, and neighbor kids become fully functional and responsible members of society. As we strive to make a positive impact on at-risk youth, we see that we must find many pieces to solve the puzzle of how to address their needs. Experience has shown me that physical training can be a critical piece of that puzzle.

Over the years, I have implemented many programs for at-risk youth. Whether in educational, recreational, therapeutic, correctional, or substance abuse prevention settings, physical training has been at the core of my approach to intervention. Over and over, I have applied the sound mind–sound body concept to concrete situations, leading to concrete results.

This book is about physical fitness and the application of physical training programs to at-risk youth. The term *at-risk* refers to those youth who by economics, family and environmental situation, or behavioral lifestyle are at-risk of developing serious problems, such as substance abuse, delinquency, dropping out of school, mental disturbances, or violence victimization. Perhaps, like me, you have puzzled over the question "How can we make a difference with such difficult problems?" A competently designed and effectively delivered physical training program can be a key part of the answer.

Yet, unfortunately, service agencies generally do not accept, encourage, or fund the use of exercise to deal with at-risk youth. Instead, at best, they usually limit the use of exercise to recreation and diversion. My experience, however, has taught me that physical training can be as critical as other educational or therapeutic strategies for not only changing health behavior but also for positively impacting values and psychological functioning. Thus, in writing this book, my goal is to provide you with a framework for justifying, designing, and delivering structured physical training programs to at-risk youth.

First, I will show you that structured physical exercise is valuable in the quest to help at-risk youth by providing you with the data to support that assertion. Second, I will provide you with the guidelines for how to implement physical training programs effectively, because any intervention will work only if you both design it competently and ensure that it is delivered by effective leaders. This is especially the case for structured exercise programs.

This material is not only based on my experience of applying physical training programs to at-risk youth, but also on a conceptual and delivery model that has proven itself over time with well-documented research. Hopefully that experience and research can help you implement your own physical training program as you seek to positively create at least one piece to solve the at-risk youth puzzle.

As you work to understand the use of physical training programs and how you should apply them, you should strive to meet the following four objectives:

1. Develop a framework for viewing the problems of at-risk youth.
2. Develop a rationale for the use of physical activity as an intervention with at-risk youth.
3. Develop an awareness of the results of others' applications of physical programs with at-risk youth.
4. Understand the guidelines for applying physical training programs to at-risk youth.

The three parts to this book will help you meet all four objectives. In the first part, I'll address the first three objectives, including an outline of and the background on the effects of physical training programs. In the second part, I'll provide you with guidelines for implementing physical training programs to meet the fourth objective. In the third part, I'll outline administrative guidelines for organizing and coordinating physical training programs.

I have written this book to assist you as you work with at-risk youth, no matter what your setting. Perhaps you work in an educational setting, such as a school-based physical education or alternative school program. Or maybe you work in a community setting, such as a Boys or Girls Club, YMCA or YWCA, city park or recreation center, a juvenile justice probation program, or a mental health or substance abuse prevention program. Or perhaps you work in a correctional, mental health, or substance abuse treatment institution. But whatever the setting, others have implemented structured physical training programs successfully in similar situations, making a positive difference in youths' lives.

This book will provide you with the information and support you need, no matter what your own personal and professional experience has been. If you have a background in physical fitness programming but lack experience working with at-risk youth, this book will provide you with the unique guidelines and frame of reference for delivering programs to at-risk youth. If you work with at-risk youth but do not have a background in physical fitness programming, this book will provide you with the guidelines you need for delivering effective physical training interventions. Either way, it will enable you to create an effective program that will be the first piece in solving the puzzle for your own community's at-risk youth.

Acknowledgments

My full appreciation of the value and effective application of exercise programs has been a developmental process. Indeed, it has been a learning and relearning experience, requiring a great deal of stamina—physically and otherwise. The material I provide in this book is based on that learning experience, which has been shared with many others—youths and adults.

The most important thing I have learned about effective physical training programs is that they are the direct result of leadership. Over the years, I have worked with many effective leaders. Space and the number of outstanding leaders do not allow me to list everyone. I will, however, name Hadley Williams and Alex Douds of the Dallas Police Department's Youth Services Program and Captains Boatman, Lawson, Weeks, and Heap of the Illinois National Guard's Operation First Choice Drug Demand Reduction program. I want to acknowledge Dr. Robert Carkhuff and Dr. Bernard Berenson for teaching me a structure for the helping process. I wish to especially commend and thank my fellow coworkers Roger Reynolds of the Cooper Institute for Aerobics Research and Jeff Sunderlin of the Illinois Department of Public Health for their sharing in my passion for this effort.

Finally, I want to recognize my wife and soul mate, Gretchen; my daughter, Jennie; and my son, Andy. Over the years, they have been my supportive "reality checks" to keep the kid in me from becoming at-risk.

Physical Training and At-Risk Youth

Part I provides the justification for using physical training programs with at-risk youth. It begins with chapter 1, which first defines the problems at-risk youth have and provides summary data that illustrate the needs of this population. It then reviews the perceptions and statistics that define who at-risk youth are and what kinds of services they need. Finally, it examines how exercise programs can meet these needs, including a perspective on the challenge of gaining acceptance of exercise programming.

Chapter 2 provides the rationale for applying physical training programs to at-risk youth. A historical and a philosophical framework is presented to guide that discussion. Documentation of research is reported that indicates the positive effects of physical training on risk factors for problem behaviors, including specific data that document the positive results of physical training programs used with at-risk problems such as substance abuse and criminal behavior. Finally, the elements of the physical domain that make physical training a unique intervention strategy are outlined.

Chapter 3 presents conclusions drawn from my experience applying physical training programs to at-risk populations in a variety of settings. Specifically, it outlines program descriptions, results, and conclusions from six major application areas, including an alcohol and drug abuse institutional program, a YMCA obesity program, a rehabilitation personal adjustment training program, a survival camp, a police diversion program, and community- and education-based substance abuse and violence prevention fitness programs.

Chapter 1

The Problems of At-Risk Youth

We had just finished the cooldown phase of the exercise class. Billy came up and said, "Hey, Doc, why is a 55-year-old white boy doing this?" Without really thinking I said, "I don't have a choice. What would happen if I didn't?" Billy said, "You'd go to pot, and [after hesitating a second] you'd start smoking pot." He laughed. "And," I said, " What happens to my head if I don't do it?" He looked me in the eye and said, "Then you wouldn't give a flip."

This is what exercise is about, especially for the at-risk kid. Billy's attitude influences his school work, his family relationships, and his functioning as a responsible member of society. Increasing physical fitness can be a valuable strategy for reversing his self-destruction.

Over the years I have been involved in implementing a variety of programs for "problem youth" in which structured physical activity has been the key element. Today, we call these kids *at-risk youth*. The terms have changed with the times, but the problems have not. Substance abuse, violence and gang behavior, juvenile crime, and poor mental health are problems that confront youth of all generations. They are symptoms of a general underlying problem, a behavioral deficit caused by the lack of a responsible and healthy lifestyle, especially the development of physical fitness.

The use of structured physical training for helping at-risk youth can make a difference. If we are serious about providing services that can change behavior, then we must address all effective strategies that impact behavior, including systematic, strenuous physical activity incorporated into education, prevention, and treatment models.

In this chapter, we'll explore who is at-risk, how Americans perceive at-risk youths' problems, and the statistics that reveal the growth of these problems. Then youth problems will be defined as behavior deficits for which solutions can be found, despite the need to address many different pieces of the problem. Finally, the rest of the chapter describes why physical training can be a useful part of the solution to at-risk problems, addressing common concerns as to its use.

Defining At-Risk Youth

The term *at-risk youth* has many connotations. Adjectives that have been applied in the past include troubled, disadvantaged, problematic, or alienated youth. I define at-risk youth as kids who live in a negative environment or lack the skills and values necessary to thrive in our society, placing them at-risk for developing serious problem behaviors, such as substance abuse, delinquency, violence, emotional disturbances, and educational and vocational difficulties.

Brendtro, Brokenleg, and Van Bockern in *Reclaiming Youth At Risk* (2) note that at-risk youth experience a common constellation of hazards that can be categorized as follows:

- Destructive relationships that lead to a health-compromising lifestyle
- Climates of futility that lead to feelings of inadequacy and fear of failure
- Learned irresponsibility that leads to a health- and community-destructive lifestyle
- Loss of purpose that leads to a self-centered, valueless lifestyle

When these hazards and potential problems are highlighted, the common response is to conclude that at-risk youth are those who live only in the inner city or rural poverty settings. The traditional notion is that these youths' physical environment, ethnicity, and socioeconomic status determine whether they are classified as at-risk. Statistics do indicate that the majority of youth classified in this manner are from minority and lower socioeconomic strata. Many youth who are at-risk for these behaviors, however, cut across ethnic and socioeconomic lines. My view of being at-risk is that a youth's behaviors, skills, values, and lifestyle are at least as important—if not more so—for determining risk status.

To some extent, you may even conclude that all youth are at-risk, given the state of our society! For example, many youth service workers in Dallas, Texas have stated that "Any kid living in Dallas is an at-risk kid." In support of that statement was an interesting opinion offered by the columnist John Leo: "We now have a culture that celebrates impulse over restraint, notoriety over achievement, rule breaking over rule keeping and any kind of incendiary expression over minimal civility" (14).

The Carnegie Corporation conducted three studies in 1989, 1992, and 1995 (5, 6, 7) to address the status and needs of American youth. All three studies showed remarkably consistent results, concluding that approximately 50% of American youth are at-risk for developing harmful behaviors. Evidently the potential problems are arising throughout the total population.

The Carnegie studies found that the adolescent period with all its stresses, peer pressure, and physical changes creates the context for many potential problems: criminal behavior, substance abuse, dropping out of school, violence victimization, unwanted pregnancy, poor health, and low levels of fitness. Moreover, the Carnegie reports asserted that such youth would become a burden to society through criminality, unemployability, and illiteracy.

Of course, the definition you choose to apply can determine whether a youth is classified as being at-risk. For example, here are two youths' situations:

> Mary comes from a single parent home in suburbia with no limits. She is free to drive around at all hours of the night. Her school has metal detectors.
>
> Alesha comes from a single parent home (parent is a drug user) with no limits. She lives in an inner city housing project and is free to roam the neighborhood at all hours of the night. Her school and apartment complex have metal detectors.

Of course, the second youth's situation has a higher probability of placing that youth at-risk for a number of serious problems. The first youth, however, is also at-risk. It is a question of degree. When we analyze substance abuse and juvenile crime statistics, we can conclude that being at-risk involves more than just socioeconomic class or living in the inner city .

The physical fitness and physical training programs described in this book have been used along the full continuum of at-risk youth from suburban school youth, to inner city youth, to incarcerated juvenile offenders. These experiences have led to the conclusion that the basic youth needs and the basic program needs are the same. And although the degree of behavioral deficits and problems may vary, requiring tailoring of program strategies, the focus should always be on encouraging the individual to be more responsible for his or her own behavior, regardless of environment or socioeconomic status.

In summary, I refuse to accept the notion that socioeconomic or ethnic status dictates the classification of "at-risk" and are the root causes that we must address. Instead, we must focus on the core needs of youth and view the root causes as a lack of the skills and values necessary to become responsible. So how do we enable youth to acquire the skills and values to develop responsibility? A structured physical training program is one major way to answer that question.

Perception of the Problem

How do Americans view the problems of at-risk children? One way to find out is to look in the *Sourcebook of Criminal Justice Statistics*. This report, produced by the U.S. Department of Justice in 1994 (4), provides prevalence and criminal justice data on a large number of areas related to youth problems. It also includes data from surveys of American citizens regarding their opinions and perceptions of crime and related problems. Some of the more interesting survey results were obtained when Americans were asked what the two most serious problems in their community were. They were rated as follows:

1. Crime and violence
2. Drug abuse

Those surveyed rated the most serious school problems (excluding financial support) as follows:

1. Drug abuse
2. Lack of discipline
3. Violence
4. Quality of education

A related survey of school-aged youth asked if they feared for their safety at school. Approximately 22% answered "yes." An additional 4.4% of surveyed youth missed at least one day of school because they felt unsafe. The most recent PRIDE (Parents Resource Institute for Drug Education; 19) survey also revealed that safety is a major concern in the schools. The report noted that 38.2% of junior high school youth reported feeling afraid another youth would hurt them in school, and 21.8% reported actually being hurt by another.

The perception that a core of causes for these community- and school-related problems exists was noted when a sample of adults were asked what they thought were the causes of violent crime among youth (4). The results were as follows:

1. Drug abuse
2. Lack of parents teaching right from wrong
3. Lack of morals and values

These perceptions gained credence from the PRIDE survey of school-aged youth (19). Approximately one third of the youth reported that their parents did not set rules or discuss issues such as drug usage. Half of the youth reported that they were not disciplined if they did break rules. Naturally, given these statistics, we can conclude that society believes that many youth are at-risk for developing a number of serious problems, which, in turn, our communities and schools must address.

The perception also exists that various social and environmental factors create these problems. For the last 50 years, both experts and laypersons alike have often cited poverty, racism, and lack of opportunity as root causes of serious youth problems. These perceptions are valid to some degree. In contrast, however, my view is that the individual factors (e.g., skills, values, individual lifestyle behaviors) are the direct causes for youth developing problems.

Regardless of our environment or socioeconomic status, we are all expected to function as responsible members of our society. Certainly, we must not waiver in demanding individual responsibility, but the process for some youth to be able to meet society's expectations may be more difficult than for others. To help these at-risk youth, we must concentrate on the individual factors as we determine which specific and concrete interventions we should make that lead to individual responsibility.

Statistics on the Problem

In moving beyond opinion, we find that the statistics support Americans' perceptions of youth problems. The statistics presented here illustrate the seriousness of the at-risk youth problem but are not exhaustive, conclusive, or definitive (in fact, many studies use different methodologies and have demonstrated a range of variation in findings).

- **Adolescent mortality.** The major causes of death are accidents, suicides, and homicides, accounting for 77% of all adolescent deaths (1).
- **Mental health.** 12% of youth under 18 have been diagnosed as having mental disorders (16). The suicide rate for adolescents increased 106% from 1970 to 1990 (4).
- **Criminal behavior and violence.** An estimated 5.5% of all youth have been arrested at least once (4). The rate of incarceration (juvenile corrections) for youth aged 17 and below has increased 6.2% from 1987 to 1991. Furthermore, 15.7% of youth report carrying a gun to school at least once, and 41% of youth have engaged in a fistfight (4). The rate of murders and manslaughter committed by juveniles increased 151% between 1976 and 1992 (4).

• **Violence victimization.** 83% of adolescents report at least one violent gang activity at their school and 23% of female adolescents report being raped or otherwise sexually assaulted (4). The rate of victimization (murder and manslaughter) for youth aged 17 and under has increased 171% from 1976 to 1992 (4).

• **Substance abuse.** The percentage of youth who have used alcohol within the last 30 days increases from 40.5% for ninth graders to 56.4% for seniors, and the percentage of youth who have used marijuana within the last 30 days increases from 13.2% for ninth graders to 22% for seniors (4). The use of "hard drugs" has reached the highest levels since the 1988–89 school year with a 36% increase in cocaine use and a 75% increase in hallucinogens (19). The percentage of all adolescents who have tried cocaine is 2.6%, and 4.5% for high school seniors (4). The rate of illicit drug use increased in the span of one year (1993 to 1994) by 45% (23). 51% of youths report that it is easy to get marijuana and 33.4% report it is easy to get cocaine (4). Total teenage drug use has increased 105% from 1992 to 1995 (12).

The Children's Defense Fund offers another perspective on the problems faced by American youth by presenting data in terms of the statistics for one day in the life of American children (8). For example, every day

9 children are murdered,

202 children are arrested for drug offenses,

307 children are arrested for crimes of violence,

340 children are arrested for drinking or drunk driving,

1,234 children run away from home,

2,255 teenagers drop out of school, and

2,350 children are in adult jails.

These statistics point out that a large number of youth engage in risky behavior. Likewise, youth are exposed to considerable risk both at school and within the community.

When we review the data collected on youth physical fitness and health, we can also make the case that American youth are at-risk for developing an unhealthy and unfit lifestyle. Dr. Ken Cooper in his book *Kid Fitness* notes the following statistics (10):

• As many as 40% of youth have at least one major cardiovascular disease risk factor (e.g., high cholesterol, high blood pressure, inactivity, or the like).

- Compared to 20 years ago, youth weigh more and have higher percents body fat.
- Only 32% of youth meet all standards for cardiovascular endurance, abdominal strength, upper body strength, and flexibility.
- By age 13, most youth have dropped out of athletics and other physical activities.

Specific data on at-risk youth populations indicate that fewer than 25% can meet fitness test standards (9). Certainly, a link between the behavioral, psychological, and social problems of youth and their physical fitness and health exists. Indeed, studies (11, 13, 21, 25) have shown that healthy behaviors tend to cluster together and unhealthy behaviors tend to cluster together. For example, health-compromising behaviors, such as unhealthy food choices, sedentary living, poor safety procedures (e.g., failure to use seat belts), cigarette smoking, illicit drug use, alcohol use, and aggressiveness, cluster together. High levels of physical activity; good nutritional habits; and absence of smoking, alcohol, and drug use tended to cluster together. In short, if a youth is at-risk, he or she is at-risk for a large number of interrelated problems.

Facing the At-Risk Puzzle

As is shown by the statistics, the extent of some of these problems among at-risk youth is large, perhaps making us feel overwhelmed. But looking at the quest for a solution as a puzzle with many pieces can help us break down the problem into manageable pieces.

The recognition that many of the at-risk youth problems such as mental health, substance abuse, and delinquency are multifaceted lifestyle problems has led to a risk factor approach for viewing such behaviors. This approach is similar to the epidemiological study of cardiovascular disease. The epidemiological approach focuses on defining the risk factors that lead to the development of cardiovascular disease. A second step of that approach is to, in turn, alter those risk factors that cause heart disease, such as smoking, lack of exercise, high cholesterol, and high blood pressure. This strategy has had a great impact on the lowering of the death rates due to cardiovascular disease.

That model is being applied to at-risk youth. Studies have evaluated patterns of problem behaviors such as substance abuse and delinquency (3, 15, 17, 18, 24) to define predictable risk patterns. Major factors that have been isolated include antisocial behavior, lack of self-esteem, maladjustment, anxiety, depression, stress, poor school attendance and performance, lack of religious beliefs, poor parental and peer relationships, early substance abuse, sensation seeking, peer and parental substance abuse, and cognitive beliefs such as having an external locus of control (feeling externally controlled by others rather than being self-directed). Defining these risk factors helps us determine the areas to impact—the pieces of the puzzle—when providing services to at-risk youth.

These well-recognized problems and risks can be, in turn, viewed as symptoms of behavioral deficits. If we define the causes of problems as behavioral deficits, it makes it possible to direct a solution toward positive behavior acquisition. My experience of dealing with at-risk youth has shown that we can conceptualize the deficits as follows:

• **A lack of life skills.** At-risk youth lack basic observation, goal setting, and planning skills to deal with their world. In many respects their world is one of disarray in which they only react as opposed to being proactive. As far back as 1976, the Texas Youth Council in a study on youthful offenders found that incarcerated youth had lower levels of physical skills (fitness), cognitive skills, and emotional skills (interpersonal skills) than youth in community diversion programs (22). In turn, the latter youth had lower skills than youth not involved in criminal activity. These statistics illustrate a continuum of skill deficits for youth who develop problems, such as criminal behavior.

• **A lack of values.** The values that consistently appear to be lacking are respect, responsibility, and self-discipline. We can see this in the lack of behaviors representative of those values.

• **A lack of citizenship.** A lack of a sense of community or obligation to the community exists.

• **A lack of a healthy lifestyle.** A simplified view of these habits is that they are the sum of behaviors that either lead toward a health-enhancing or a health-compromising lifestyle. Perry and Jessor (20) noted that the issue of health revolves around four areas: physical health, psychological health, social health (social effectiveness), and personal health (individual potential). They found that an individual youth's health areas cluster either for better (health-enhancing in all four areas) or for worse (health-compromising in all four areas). It appears that at most levels the at-risk youth lifestyle is health-compromising. The traits that commonly appear as deficits that negatively influence all four health areas are the following:

• A lack of delay of gratification
• A pursuit of expediency
• Self-indulgence

- Passive observation of the environment
- Irresponsibility
- Avoidance of challenge or discomfort
- Lack of self-esteem and self-confidence

In defining at-risk youth problems as having a core of deficit risk factors, the issue then becomes one of defining and implementing strategies to reverse these deficits.

Defining the Pieces of the At-Risk Youth Puzzle

When we examine the statistics regarding the extent of at-risk youth problems, it becomes clear that we are not always making the interventions that help youth develop the skills and values required to be responsible citizens. Physical training leading to fitness can be a powerful tool in the effort to make more effective interventions.

I have talked to many workers in the field who have felt, at times, like throwing in the towel in exasperation at the extent of at-risk youths' problems. Those feelings are echoed by a youth service worker in a Chicago inner city community recreation center who, when asked how he handles the kids, said, "When in doubt about what to do, we play dodgeball."

Unfortunately, we must deal with the at-risk puzzle with more creativity than playing dodgeball. Yet, it often is unclear what the major causes of the problems are and what the solutions should be. I can recall many meetings with helping staff from a variety of agencies (education, juvenile justice, mental health, substance abuse) in which we would struggle to define what the pieces of the puzzle should be. I often heard "We don't know what works and we don't know how to measure it." Naturally, it's discouraging when many conclude that no solution to this puzzle exists. Yet, there is a way to put the puzzle together if we view it one piece at a time, looking for how one piece can lead to another.

Experts in the fields of education, substance abuse, juvenile delinquency, and mental health have defined a variety of those pieces for us, including parenting training, self-awareness training, life skills training, values training, basic educational skills, cognitive restructuring, peer pressure reversal, and punishment. One other important piece exists: physical training leading to increased physical fitness.

The Physical Training Piece of the Puzzle

A simplified way to categorize the pieces of the puzzle is to define the physical, emotional, and intellectual needs of at-risk youth and develop interventions to meet those needs. In the past, the physical domain has received little attention. However, systematic physical training actually can aid in meeting needs in all three areas of deficits: physical, emotional, and intellectual.

The concept of physical training presented here doesn't mean recreation, free time, or sport participation. Those who work with at-risk youth usually implement these informal forms of physical activity as support, rather than core, programs. In contrast, systematic physical training is focused activity designed to increase physical fitness that can be applied as the core of an intervention program.

But what exactly is physical fitness? Physical fitness is the direct result of undergoing strenuous exercise. It is composed of four basic elements:

1. **Cardiovascular endurance**, or aerobic power, is the circulatory system's ability to transport oxygen, giving you the stamina to perform endurance activity. In addition, maintaining this fitness area can help control obesity and prevent heart disease and diabetes—all important health considerations. Examples of activities that develop cardiovascular endurance include distance running, swimming, and racquetball.

2. **Strength** can be broken down into absolute muscular strength (the ability of a muscle to generate force) and muscular endurance (the ability to make repeated contractions). Naturally, many physical activities require power and repetitive muscle movements. Moreover, maintaining adequate strength can enhance health by helping to prevent many orthopedic injuries, back problems, and osteoporosis. Examples of activities that help develop absolute muscular strength and muscular endurance include weight training and calisthenics.

3. **Flexibility** refers to the ranges of motion in the joints, or the ability to stretch, bend, and twist, affecting the performance of fluid activity. Flexibility has many health benefits in terms of injury prevention, especially for the low back. Examples of activities that develop flexibility include stretching exercises and gymnastics.

4. **Body composition** is often referred to as percent body fat. It affects appearance and physical performance as well as many health aspects. Excessive body fat is a risk factor for many cardiovascular and metabolic

diseases. Exercise that utilizes many calories, such as running, walking, and swimming, can help decrease body fat.

You can use the exercise process not only to increase fitness but also to develop positive social values, such as self-discipline and responsibility, as well as life skills, such as goal setting and planning. It also can have a bearing on many psychological factors, such as the development of self-esteem and well-being and the lessening of anxiety and depression.

The Value of Physical Training for At-Risk Youth

My experience with at-risk youth has led me to conclude that they often define themselves as victims. The victim mentality is one in which the individual is always reacting and responding as opposed to initiating and acting. Some at-risk youth, however, appear to have initiative and purpose. Examples include some gang youth and apparently successful youthful offenders—until they get caught. These youth, however, are in the minority. You could even make the argument that most of these youth are only denying their feelings of victimization. Initiating daily, intense exercise is one simple behavior that helps reduce these feelings—no matter how we choose to define "victim."

Why do youth so easily feel victimized? We have become a passive, consuming society with ample opportunity for instant gratification and immediate avoidance of life's discomforts. Not surprisingly, the members of our society often fail to learn values such as self-reliance, self-discipline, delay of gratification, and tolerance of discomfort. As a consequence, we succumb to the stresses of modern living. This is especially devastating for at-risk youth.

Physical exercise can provide some purpose and meaning in an environment in which often none exist. Indeed, the purpose of focused exercise is to reach a goal, to do what you set out to do. This is what discipline is all about. The physical domain is one of the few areas in modern life in which we can experience a concrete and honest reality check. Thus, the daily workout becomes an exercise in self-control and self-discipline. Exercise provides a daily dose of control over your environment, even if the rest of your life is in complete disarray.

The meaning of that exercise is in the process, the movement, and the physiological and psychological feelings that occur. The intensity of exercise lets us know we are alive. The results let us know we are worth it. Contrary to current psychological thought, I believe action precedes insight. The learning of purpose and meaning through exercise is the laboratory for learning the purpose and meaning of life: The learning is in the doing.

Yet, employing physical training programs to help at-risk youth is not the complete solution to the puzzle. We must meet many other emotional, intellectual, and behavioral needs. Still, involving youth in a systematic physical training program can prepare them for more in-depth and expansive prevention and treatment. Certainly, youth can have more energy, discipline, and self-confidence to commit to other interventions by undergoing the physical training process. Through physical training, you can help youth establish the basis for further growth. Thus, a physical training program is not only a piece of the puzzle but the first piece to which you and the youth can add other pieces.

The Challenge of Promoting Physical Training as an Effective Intervention

The at-risk puzzle is this: How do we develop at-risk youth so that they engage in a constructive lifestyle? The piece of that puzzle that is defined in this book is the use of systematic physical training to increase physical fitness.

This is not always an easy task! A major challenge is that many of those in the helping professions see physical training as just a physical health or recreation process. Physical exercise as a tool for health promotion and disease prevention or as leisure time recreation are valid missions for physical activity programs. But when we look at the problems facing at-risk youth today, health promotion and disease prevention are not the most critical issues. We need to create exercise activities that teach youth to deal with the problems that are killing them, such as substance abuse and violence.

The established helping fields of psychology, counseling, education, and social work, which provide the majority of services to at-risk youth, tend to be completely unfamiliar with the physical domain or the benefits of applying exercise beyond leisure time recreation. This is a major challenge to instituting physical training programs. An interview I had with a research psychologist concerning an expansion of an at-risk physical training program called "First Choice" highlighted this fact.

Prior to the interview, the psychologist had been given evaluation reports showing many positive results of past applications of First Choice on fitness and substance abuse changes in inner city youth. As part of the interview, he observed a class of such youth participating in the First Choice exercise activities. The initial focus of his comments was on how the theoretical model behind the program did not address minority issues. Then, he repeatedly made the point that the psychological literature suggested that such youth do not respond to these types of exercise programs. Furthermore, he was concerned that the program didn't address self-esteem enough, even though substance use had decreased. Finally, he was concerned over the positive results of the program, leading to funding for the expansion of First Choice. He stated, "My concern is that the fitness program may be working and, if so, then needed psychological counseling programs would not get the funding." When I asked him his experience in working with inner city youth, he said he had done some research but no hands-on delivery of services. When I asked him if his counseling programs have any data to support that they work, he replied that they can't really be measured.

His perception and beliefs were an example of many interactions I have had over the years. He denied his own observations of minority youth actually participating. He denied evaluation data that did not fit his framework. He denied the importance of the bottom line (reduced substance abuse) and, instead, emphasized concern over a theoretical construct such as self-esteem. But most importantly of all, he denied what the program was all about: helping the kids. All of his perceptions were based on theory and literature, not on the real-world experience of having to deliver a service and make an impact.

In order to meet the challenge of at-risk youth, we must deliver effective programs. Recent cutbacks in school physical education illustrate why. Cutbacks were made not because physical education has no value, but because, too often, physical education has not been delivered effectively. The same is true for the use of physical training to help improve at-risk youth behavior: Physical training will only affect physical fitness and other changes in at-risk youth behavior if valid programs are delivered by effective fitness leaders.

Conclusion

At-risk youth are those youth who live in a negative environment or lack life skills and values, placing them at-risk for developing serious problem behaviors, such as substance abuse, delinquency, violence, emotional disturbances, and educational and vocational difficulties. Not all at-risk youth are at-risk for the same reasons. But no matter what the problems and the causes are, the perceptions and statistics clearly indicate large numbers of youths are not developing into responsible adults. Thus, they are at-risk for developing serious problems.

Structured physical training or exercise can be a unique domain in which to address many of the problems of at-risk youth. To meet the needs of this target group, physical training that develops physical fitness can be a valuable program in your intervention efforts.

References

1. Blum, R. 1987. Contemporary threats to adolescent health in the United States. *Journal of the American Medical Association* 257(24):3390-3395.

2. Brendtro, L., M. Brokenleg, and S. Van Bockern. 1990. *Reclaiming youth at risk*. Bloomington, IN: National Education Service.

3. Bry, B., P. McKeon, and R. Pandina. 1982. Extent of drug use as a function of number of risk factors. *Journal of Abnormal Psychology* 91:273-279.

4. Bureau of Justice Statistics. 1994. *Sourcebook of criminal justice statistics*. Washington, DC: U.S. Department of Justice, Government Printing Office.

5. Carnegie Council on Adolescent Development. 1989. *Turning points: Preparing American youth for the 21st century*. New York: The Carnegie Corporation.

6. ———. 1992. *A matter of time*. New York: The Carnegie Corporation.

7. ———. 1995. *Great transitions*. New York: The Carnegie Corporation.

8. Children's Defense Fund. 1994. *The state of America's children yearbook*. Washington, DC: Children's Defense Fund.

9. Collingwood, T., R. Reynolds, H.W. Kohl, S. Sloan, and W. Smith. 1991. Physical fitness effects on substance abuse risk factors and use patterns: A preliminary study. *Journal of Drug Education* 21(1):73-84.

10. Cooper, K. 1991. *Kid fitness*. New York: Bantam Books.

11. Hars, R., A. Stacy, and M. DeMatteo. 1984. Covariation among health-related behaviors. *Addictive Behavior* 9(3):315-318.

12. Health and Human Services. 1996. *National household survey on drug abuse*. Washington, DC: U.S. Health and Human Services, Government Printing Office.

13. Jessor, R. 1989. The health of youth: A behavioral science perspective. Paper read at the WHO Conference on the Health of Youth, Geneva, Switzerland.

14. Leo, J. 1996. Gutter talk! *Dallas Morning News*, 4/17/96, p. 29A.

15. Mayer, J. 1988. The personality characteristics of adolescents who use and misuse alcohol. *Adolescence XXIII* 90:383-404.

16. National Institute of Mental Heath. 1990. *National plan for research on child and adolescent mental health disorders*. Washington, DC: U.S. Health and Human Services, Government Printing Office.

17. Newcomb, M., E. Maddahian, and B. Bentler. 1986. Risk factors for drug use among adolescents. *American Journal of Public Health* 76(5):525-531.

18. Oetting, E., and F. Beauvais. 1984. Common elements in youth drug abuse: Peer clusters and other psychosocial factors. *Journal of Drug Issues* 74:668-672.

19. PRIDE. 1995. *The 1995 PRIDE survey of drug abuse.* Atlanta: PRIDE, Inc.

20. Perry, C., and R. Jessor. 1985. The concept of health promotion and the prevention of adolescent drug abuse. *Health Education Quarterly* 12(2):169-184.

21. Stocker, H., T. Retschald, J. Sollberger, R. Gass, and T. Abelin. 1978. Influencing factors related to narcotic consumption and leisure sports in juveniles. *Soz Praventivmed* 23(4):246-247.

22. Texas Youth Council. 1976. *Master plan for the state of Texas.* Austin, TX: Texas Youth Council.

23. U.S. Public Health Service. 1995. *Trends in substance use: 1979–1994.* Washington, DC: U.S. Health and Human Services, Government Printing Office.

24. Veneziano, C., and L. Veneziano. 1987. MMPI profiles among institutionalized male delinquents. *Child Psychiatry and Human Development* 18:95-102.

25. Winnail, S., R. Valois, R. McKeown, R. Saunders, and R. Pate. 1995. Relationship between physical activity level and cigarette, smokeless tobacco and marijuana use. *Journal of School Health* 65(10):438-442.

Chapter 2

The Rationale for Physical Training Programs

When it comes to the problem of at-risk youth, the statistical data and the perceptions of the public agree. Our youth have serious problems, whether we live and work in the inner city, the suburbs, or the country. The issue is not so much one of defining the causes of these problems but of finding and organizing the pieces of the puzzle to reduce the risks for youth.

In exploring strategies to overcome the youth deficits we discussed in chapter 1, we can readily see that our focus must be on meeting youth needs by providing them with opportunities to develop skills and values that, in turn, enable them to reduce their deficits. Carkhuff and Berenson have shown that the model of "training as treatment" is a valuable strategy for helping youth function better in counseling, educational, and vocational programs (4). Their model is built on the idea that teaching skills to overcome deficits is a valuable treatment mode— just as counseling and psychotherapy are. Their work supports my assertion that physical training is one healthy activity that can help at-risk youth alter risk factors and reduce deficits.

The main focus of this chapter is to describe reasons why physical training works as an at-risk youth intervention tool and to justify its use with both historical precedents and current studies that show it significantly reduces risk and youth problems. It concludes with a description of the attributes of the physical domain that make physical training especially effective.

The Basic Physical Training Rationale

What, specifically, is the rationale for implementing physical training programs? First, we know that physical training increases physical fitness, which is more than enough reason to provide exercise programs to at-risk youth. However, my experience in getting programs accepted and installed has shown that more justification is needed.

We can view the various problems that at-risk youth are susceptible to as developmental behavior problems. In other words, the extent to which problems emerge is due, in part, to the developmental aspects of adolescence and how well a youth overcomes deficits during that developmental period. We can consider the decisions that youth have to make at the adolescent stage as the many behavioral crossroads of teenage life. Physical training programs can be valuable tools to help youth deal with these challenges. A framework for looking at this assertion with supporting data has been developed by others, including Brendtro, Brokenleg, and Van Bockern (2) and Jessor (23). Their framework can be summarized as follows:

1. Risky behavior, such as substance abuse or criminal behavior, is not an isolated behavior but an integrated component of a health-compromising behavior cluster or syndrome.

2. The adolescent faces the difficult challenges of developmental choices between health-enhancing or health-compromising behaviors in regard to physical, social, and psychological aspects of health.

3. Adolescence is a high-risk stage of life for developing a health-compromising lifestyle. This is when youth choose between health-compromising and health-enhancing lifestyles. We can view various behaviors developed during adolescence as interrelated and leaning toward one or the other lifestyle (syndrome).

4. Many developmental themes influence that choice, including

   • a search for identity,
   • the development of a sense of autonomy,
   • the development of a sense of self-control,
   • the development of a sense of accomplishment,
   • the development of the concept of delayed gratification,
   • the development of strategies to reduce physical and psychological pain,
   • peer pressure, and
   • stress.

5. We can view risky behavior as attempts to address those themes. The problem is that such behavior produces a false sense of

security in dealing with those issues: In essence, it is an avoidance behavior.

Given this developmental view of behavioral problems, the intervention goals evolve naturally:

1. A goal of intervention is to enable youth to develop a healthy lifestyle. Intervention should emphasize the health-enhancing cluster of behaviors.

2. A goal of intervention should be to replace health-compromising behaviors with health-enhancing behaviors.

3. A goal of intervention should be to focus on those skills and values that equip youth with a health-enhancing lifestyle to serve as an alternative to the health-compromising lifestyle.

With this perspective, physical training serves as a concrete intervention that teaches youth how to create the health-enhancing lifestyle.

During the last decade, experts have tended to define many social problems, such as crime and violence, as public health problems. A public health approach to any health problem focuses upon three components of a disease process: the agent causing the disease, the environment, and the host (the person who is susceptible). We can rework this model to define strategies for helping at-risk youth avoid the health-compromising lifestyle (the disease).

- **Neutralizing the agent.** For example, find ways to alter the substance of drugs and alcohol (the agent) so that they are not as health-compromising.

- **Controlling the environment.** For example, make schools secure enough so that violence cannot occur.

- **Immunizing the host.** For example, influence the behaviors and lifestyles of youth (the host) so they will not try drugs or be involved in criminal behavior.

The strategy presented here is to use exercise to "immunize the host." To overcome deficits, exercise is a natural tool for teaching life skills, values, citizenship, and a healthy lifestyle. By overcoming deficits, we help youth reduce their risk factors. Participating in regular, strenuous exercise can set the stage for developing a health-enhancing lifestyle. With a health-enhancing lifestyle, a youth has a lower risk of developing serious problems.

Using Physical Training to Reduce the Risk

Physical training has a long history in Western civilization, not only as a means to improving fitness but also as a mental discipline that builds character. Today, though, we can support the use of training as a path to better behavior with data from studies that show it works.

The Physical Fitness Philosophy

Currently, most experts in the field emphasize the health-promoting value of physical training, but historically, we have viewed it as a method of developing self-discipline as well. In turn, we have viewed that self-discipline as providing the basis for character development. This concept is best illustrated by America's acceptance of the "work ethic." Since the founding of this nation, society at large has held the implicit belief that if we practice self-discipline and make sacrifices through self-control, we will "get ahead."

For example, prior to the recent health justification for fitness and exercise, America's fitness mission was aimed at the development of good citizenship. A major rationale for fitness was to prepare youth to serve their country. From 1917 to the 1960s a major theme of fitness was to ensure the military preparedness of the nation. A parallel theme was the importance of fitness for performing physical work. The initial studies of the Harvard Fatigue Laboratory, for example, were aimed at defining the fitness required to perform work tasks and to perform in a variety of athletic endeavors. Both of these rationales were based on a work ethic.

Physical activity as a means for developing morals and values is best explained by reviewing the original report of the President's Council on Youth Fitness, published in 1958 (40). This report served as the blueprint for the establishment of the President's Council on Physical Fitness and Sports and for a national mission to increase the physical activity and fitness of Americans. Although nearly 40 years old, the report has much to say about the challenges we face as a nation today and the value of physical activity to meet those challenges.

The report detailed the youth problems of 20th-century society as follows (40, p. 32):

- We have become a nation concerned with "nurturing comfort."
- We are self-indulgent to the extreme.
- We have no concept of delay of gratification.

- We are passive observers as opposed to active participants.
- We "buy, watch, and receive" rather than "do, make, and create."

The point is that 20th-century urban society sets the scene for the development of a negative lifestyle. Physical activity may be the only means to counteract those influences. The process of getting fit fosters delay of gratification and an active approach to life, instilling in youth a basis for survival in 20th-century society. Only now, we must focus on surviving the 21st century.

The report elaborated on how physical activity is the direct means by which we can help youth build self-reliance and citizenship. Physical activity is a method for developing individual responsibility, impacting character beyond that of mere physical performance. Strenuous physical activity is also a vehicle for instilling duty, obligation, and responsibility inherent in citizenship. You start with a duty to yourself (developing fitness to instill the duty concept), followed by duty to serve your country and your fellow man.

Certainly, the reasons for and value of a physically active lifestyle have a strong historical and philosophical background, clearly defining the rationale for using physical training with at-risk youth. To fully understand that rationale, however, we must look at the data.

Physical Training and Risk Factors

While historical and philosophical rationales for utilizing physical training with at-risk youth exist, the argument for its application must come from the data that support the effects of physical training. Evaluations of physical training programs have shown strenuous exercise to have a positive impact on many of the risk factors and deficits associated with at-risk youth. Data also support a strong relationship between levels of physical fitness and levels of risk factors. Figure 2.1 summarizes several studies that have documented physical training effects.

These results document that a relationship between exercise and many psychological and social risk factors exists. Indeed, these data support the assertion that many potential benefits of applying physical exercise to other areas of functioning related to at-risk youths' problems are possible.

The evidence is gradually gaining acceptance within the fields outside of exercise science. The National Institute for Mental Health (NIMH) consensus panel emphasized the beneficial emotional effect of exercise across all ages and for both sexes and recommended its application as a prevention and treatment strategy (30).

Increased self-esteem and self-concept (6, 17, 19)
Increased feelings of well-being (7, 8, 14, 29, 32)
Increased emotional stability (1, 19)
Increased school attendance (8, 14)
Increased academic or vocational training performance (6, 8, 14)
Increased positive parental relationships (7)
Increased responsibility (8, 15, 16)
Increased levels of life skills (9, 11, 14)
Decreased depression (17, 19, 24, 28)
Decreased anxiety (1, 24, 37)
Decreased perception of stress (3, 32)

Figure 2.1 Summary of studies showing physical training's effect on risk factors and skill deficits.

Physical Training and Specific At-Risk Youth Problems

In several studies, researchers have investigated the effects of physical training on specific at-risk youth problems, including emotionally disturbed, delinquent, and substance abuse behavior.

- **Effects on emotionally disturbed behavior.** Studies have shown reduction in symptoms with the application of physical training. This has especially been noted for depressed patients (6, 18, 24, 28).
- **Effects on delinquent behavior.** The utilization of physical training both within institutional and community settings has shown a positive effect on reducing criminal offenses and related delinquent behavior (9, 10, 11, 22, 26).
- **Effects on substance abuse behavior.** Applications of physical training to alcoholics have been shown to help reduce consumption (20, 31, 34, 38). Likewise, evaluations of physical training programs used with drug abusers have shown significant decreases in multiple drug usage as well as increases in abstinence (7, 8, 12, 13, 14, 41).

Of interest is that these studies reflect the full application of physical training programs across a spectrum of settings, including the following:

Education   Junior high and senior high physical education classes

	Alternative school physical education
	After-school activity sessions
	Drug and health education classes
Community recreation	YMCA and YWCA classes
	Boys Club and Girls Club classes
	City recreation center classes
Juvenile justice	Community-based probation service programs
	Police diversion and recreation programs
	Correctional institution programs
Social services	Community mental health counseling programs
	Refugee relocation service programs
	Neighborhood youth service agencies
	Rehabilitation programs
Substance abuse	Community-based prevention programs
	Community counseling agencies
	Institutional treatment centers

While these studies did not address the specific causes for these changes, some speculations have been made. MacMahon (25) outlined the possible mechanisms by which exercise could have an impact on risk factors and problem behaviors to include psychological (self-control and mastery, deep relaxation and recreational distraction, feedback training) and physiological theories (alterations in neurotransmitters and endorphin levels). Another view is that developing a health-enhancing lifestyle establishes a pattern into which health-compromising behaviors do not fit.

Whatever the reasons, the data from these studies—gathered from real-world fitness program applications, not simply theory and philosophy—all suggest that physical training can be a valuable intervention strategy to directly influence problem behavior.

The Uniqueness of the Physical Domain

The effects of physical training reflected in the studies stem from the unique qualities of the process of exercise. The data provide solid evidence that the physical domain can be a valid teaching domain for helping youth develop many deficit areas to, in turn, affect risk factors and problem behaviors. Why? What is unique about strenuous physical activity, making it a valuable tool? To answer, we have to view physical activity as both a process and an outcome.

As a process, the physical domain is uniquely suited as a teaching domain in that systematic physical training has the following characteristics:

- It is a very concrete and specific process.
- It is an honest process, making distortions difficult.
- It is goal-oriented.
- It is active, not passive.
- It requires both leaders and followers.
- It is demanding, perhaps involving discomfort.
- Results are delayed.
- It can be a highly disciplined activity.
- It requires respect for others.

The outcomes of participation can involve other benefits beyond the risk factor and behavior changes we've already discussed, including

- the development of a health-enhancing lifestyle,
- increased physical fitness,
- increased self-confidence,
- increased self-discipline,
- increased sense of personal responsibility,
- increased willingness to address developmental problems, and
- increased ability to set goals and make systematic plans to reach goals.

We can view the result of participation in strenuous exercise as a step-by-step process leading to behavioral changes, which then help at-risk youth deal with many of their problems (see figure 2.2).

The process and outcome of exercise cannot be duplicated as directly by counseling or by sit-down educational classes. Exercise, unfortunately, has not always been accepted or utilized to take full advantage of the learning that may take place within the physical domain.

Although studies support the value of using structured exercise programs to address the needs of at-risk youth, some individuals in the field believe that at-risk youth do not respond to this type of highly structured, disciplined approach. The data as well as my experience in

1. Exercise participation leads to the development of a health-enhancing lifestyle.

2. The health-enhancing lifestyle leads to increased physical fitness.

3. Increased physical fitness leads to self-confidence.

4. Increased self-confidence leads to self-discipline and control.

5. Increased self-discipline leads to an ability to set goals and to plan to meet them.

6. Increased goal setting and planning leads to increased responsibility.

7. Increased responsibility leads to a readiness to address at-risk problems.

Figure 2.2   Process leading to behavioral changes.

implementing such programs, however, suggest the opposite. Evaluation studies of the application of voluntary physical training programs lasting from 12 to 16 weeks consistently report attendance rates between 75% and 98% (8, 9, 14).

At-risk youth are seeking positive sources of structure and discipline in their lives. In addition to the high attendance rates noted, the fact that youth in the inner cities are seeking to enroll in parochial schools and to participate in Junior ROTC attests to this. Anecdotal data (9, 27) have shown that at-risk youth are looking for clear rules and discipline as well as positive role models, and they want to participate in programs or belong to organizations that give them direction and are located in the neighborhood. You can design effective and structured physical training programs to meet these expectations as reflected by good participation and attendance.

The value of physical training programing is also seen when it is compared to other interventions aimed at at-risk youth. We can readily see many common denominators. For example, summary studies evaluating the effects of substance abuse and delinquency prevention programs indicate that programs that emphasize skill learning, responsibility, and accountability for behavior, goal setting, planning, and alternative lifestyle activities, such as physical activity, are the ones that have the most success (21, 33, 36, 39). These are the same characteristics that can be the focus of a structured exercise and physical fitness program.

Physical training programs are only part of the answer to meet the needs of at-risk youth. But getting youth involved in a systematic physical training program can prepare them for more in-depth and expansive prevention and treatment. By undergoing the physical training process, youth can have more energy, discipline, and self-confidence to commit themselves to other interventions. In effect, the physical training process establishes a base for helping youth create meaning and purpose in their lives.

Conclusion

The Carnegie Council on Adolescent Development report suggests that increasing health and fitness can be a major tool for helping youth in all of the at-risk problem areas (5). From a purely physiological perspective, the need to address the physical fitness needs of at-risk youth is great. Indeed, physical fitness is a basic need for all youth, but when we look at the other needs of at-risk youth and the exercise benefits that can occur, the value of physical training becomes even more important. This is because physical training can directly impact the risk factors and the problem behaviors associated with at-risk youth. There is historical, philosophical, and research support for this rationale.

No matter our opinions as to the nature of at-risk youth problems, if we are serious about affecting at-risk youth for the better, then we must look at the bottom line: youth developing more responsible lifestyles. Do our kids develop a lifestyle that "immunizes" them from using drugs and committing crimes, but at the same time gives them the confidence and skills to reach their full potentials? The data as well as my experience say that implementing systematic physical exercise programs has great potential for answering this question with a resounding "Yes!"

The former Chairman of the President's Council on Physical Fitness and Sports, the late George Allen, created a poster entitled "What Is a Workout?" that captures the essence of the uniqueness and value of the physical domain (35). His statements give us very personal and direct conclusions, summarizing the rationale for physical training.

" What Is a Workout?

- A workout is 25% **PERSPIRATION** and 75% **DETERMINATION**. Stated another way, it is 1 part physical exertion and 3 parts self-discipline. Doing it is easy once you get started.
- A workout makes you better today than you were yesterday. It strengthens the body, relaxes the mind, and **toughens the spirit**.

When you work out regularly, your problems diminish and your **confidence** grows.

- A workout is a personal triumph over laziness and procrastination. It is the badge of a **WINNER**—the mark of an organized, goal-oriented person who has taken change of his, or her, destiny.

- A workout is a wise use of time and an **INVESTMENT in excellence**. It is a way of preparing for life's challenges and proving to yourself that you have what it takes to do what is necessary.

- A workout is a key that helps to unlock the door to OPPORTUNITY and SUCCESS. Hidden within each of us is an extraordinary force. **Physical and mental fitness are the triggers** that can release it.

- A workout is a form of REBIRTH. When you finish a good workout, you don't simply feel better. **YOU FEEL BETTER ABOUT YOURSELF.** "

Courtesy of The President's Council on Physical Fitness and Sports.

References

1. Blumenthal, J., R. Williams, T. Needels, and A. Wallace. 1982. Psychological changes accompanying aerobic exercise in healthy middle aged adults. *Psychosomatic Medicine* 44:529-536.

2. Brendtro, L., M. Brokenleg, and S. Van Bockern. 1990. *Reclaiming youth at-risk*. Bloomington, IN: National Education Service.

3. Brown, J., and J. Siegel. 1988. Exercise as a buffer for life stresses. *Health Psychology* 7(4):341-353.

4. Carkhuff, R., and B. Berenson. 1976. *Teaching as treatment*. Amherst, MA: Human Resource Development Press.

5. Carnegie Council on Adolescent Development. 1989. *Turning points: Preparing American youth for the 21st century*. New York: The Carnegie Corporation.

6. Collingwood, T. 1972. The effects of physical training upon behavior and self attitudes. *Journal of Clinical Psychology* 283:71-75.

7. ———. 1992. *Fitness intervention training: An evaluation of the installation of physical fitness programs for substance abuse prevention and treatment*. Springfield, IL: Illinois Department of Alcohol and Substance Abuse.

8. ———. 1996. *The effects of Operation First Choice drug demand reduction initiative: A program evaluation*. Springfield, IL: Illinois National Guard.

9. Collingwood, T., A. Douds, H. Williams, and R. Wilson. 1979. *Developing youth resources*. Amherst, MA: Human Resource Development Press.

10. Collingwood, T., and M. Englesjgerd. 1977. Physical fitness, delinquency, and delinquency prevention. *Journal of Health, Physical Education, Recreation and Dance* 48(6):23.

11. Collingwood, T., and B. Genthner. 1980. Skills training as treatment for juvenile delinquents. *Professional Psychology* 11:591-598.

12. Collingwood, T., R. Reynolds, B. Jester, and D. DeBord. 1992. Enlisting physical education for the war on drugs. *Journal of Physical Education, Recreation and Dance* 63(2):25-28.

13. Collingwood, T., R. Reynolds, H.W. Kohl, S. Sloan, and W. Smith. 1991. Physical fitness effects on substance abuse risk factors and use patterns: A preliminary study. *Journal of Drug Education* 21(1):73-84.

14. Collingwood, T., J. Sunderlin, and H.W. Kohl. 1994. The use of a staff training model for implementing fitness programming to prevent substance abuse with at-risk youth. *American Journal of Health Promotion* 9(1):20-23.

15. Compagnone, N. 1995. Teaching responsibility to rural elementary youth. *Journal of Physical Education, Recreation and Dance* 66(6):58-63.

16. DeBusk, M., and D. Hellison. 1989. Implementing physical education self-responsibility model for delinquency prone youth. *Journal of Teaching in Physical Education* 8(2):104-112.

17. Doan, R., and A. Schernan. 1987. The therapeutic effect of physical fitness on measures of personality: A literature review. *Journal of Counseling and Development* 66:28-35.

18. Doyne, E., D. Chambless, and L. Beutler. 1982. Aerobic exercise as a treatment for depression in women. *Behavior Therapy* 14:434-440.

19. Folkins, C., and W. Sime. 1981. Physical fitness training and mental health. *American Psychologist* 36(4):373-389.

20. Gary, V., and D. Guthrie. 1982. The effect of jogging on physical fitness and self-concept in hospitalized alcoholics. *Quarterly Journal Studies in Alcoholism* 29:292-303.

21. Hawkins, J., R. Catalano, and E. Wells. 1986. Measuring effects of skills training interventions for drug abusers. *Journal of Clinical Psychology* 54(5):661-664.

22. Hilyer, J., D. Wilson, and C. Dillon. 1982. Physical fitness training and counseling as treatment for youthful offenders. *Journal of Counseling Psychology* 33:1073-1078.

23. Jessor, R. 1989. The health of youth: A behavioral science perspective. Paper presented at the WHO Conference on the Health of Youth, Geneva, Switzerland.

24. Kugler, J., H. Seelbach, and G. Kruskemper. 1994. Effects of rehabilitation exercise program on anxiety and depression in coronary patients: A meta-analysis. *British Journal of Clinical Psychology* 33(3):401-410.

25. MacMahon, J. 1990. The psychological benefits of exercise and the treatment of delinquent adolescents. *Sports Medicine* 9(6):344-351.

26. MacMahon, J., and R. Gross. 1988. Physical and psychological effects of aerobic exercise in delinquent adolescent males. *Journal of Diseases of Children* 142:1361-1366.

27. McLaghlin, M., M. Irby, and J. Langman. 1994. *Urban sanctuaries*. San Francisco: Jossey-Bass.

28. Martinsen, J. 1990. Benefits of exercise for the treatment of depression. *Sports Medicine* 9(6):380-389.

29. Morgan, W., and S. Goldston, ed. 1987. *Exercise and mental health*. New York: Hemisphere Press.

30. Morgan, W., and P. O'Connor. 1988. Exercise and mental health. In *Exercise adherence*, ed. R. Dishman, 91-106. Champaign, IL: Human Kinetics.

31. Murphy, T., R. Pagano, and G. Marlatt. 1986. Lifestyle modification with heavy alcohol drinkers: Effects of aerobic exercise and meditation. *Addictive Behavior* 11:175-186.

32. Norris, R., D. Carroll, and R. Cochrane. 1990. The effects of aerobic and anaerobic training on fitness, blood pressure, psychological stress and well being. *Psychosomatic Research* 34(4):367-375.

33. Perry, C. 1987. Results of prevention programs with adolescents. *Drug and Alcohol Dependency* 20 (September):13-19.

34. Palmer, J. 1994. Impact of aerobic exercise on inpatient alcoholism treatment. *Directions in Clinical Psychology* 4(Spring):1-4.

35. President's Council on Physical Fitness and Sports. 1983. *What is a workout?* Washington, DC: Government Printing Office.

36. Romig, D. 1978. *Justice for our children*. Lexington, MA: Lexington Books.

37. Steptoe, A., and S. Cox. 1988. Acute effects of aerobic exercise on mood. *Health Psychology* 7(4):329-340.

38. Sinyor, D., T. Brown, L. Rostant, and P. Seraganian. 1982. The role of a physical program in the treatment of alcoholism. *Journal of Studies on Alcohol* 43:380-386.

39. Tobler, N. 1987. Meta-analysis of 143 adolescent drug prevention programs: Quantitative outcome results of program participants compared to a control and comparison group. *Journal of Drug Issues* 16:537-567.

40. U.S. Department of Health, Education and Welfare. 1958. *Fitness of American youth*. Washington, DC: Government Printing Office.

41. Winnail, S., R. Valois, R. McKeown, R. Saunders, and R. Pate. Relationship between physical activity level and cigarette, smokeless tobacco and marijuana use. *Journal of School Health* 65(10):438-442.

Chapter 3

Lessons From the Application of Physical Training Programs

The conclusion that physical training is of value for meeting the needs of at-risk youth is only valid if it is based on reality. In other words, even though it sounds good, does it really work that way? Data have certainly documented the value of such efforts. Experience, however, is the best teacher.

My awareness of the value of physical training has developed over the last 30 years through personally developing and delivering exercise-based education, prevention, and treatment programs for at-risk populations at over 60 different sites. Those applications can be categorized into six different settings or program areas, covering a variety of situations. The learning from each application served as a foundation for the next one, with each experience contributing new insights that helped me define the important elements of a successful physical fitness training program.

In this chapter, I'll relate the details of implementing the various physical training programs, outlining the lessons learned from those experiences, thereby giving you a broader perspective on how to implement a physical training program for at-risk youth. Each of the six application settings is presented with an overview of the situation, a description of the program, the results from the program, and the learnings from the application of the program.

Veterans Administration Alcohol Rehabilitation Program

I first used physical training for other than physical fitness purposes over 25 years ago during an internship for a doctorate in psychology.

Because I was a veteran, I was initially assigned to assist in group therapy for 10 to 15 alcohol- and drug-abusing patients in the Buffalo (New York) Veterans Administration Hospital alcohol rehabilitation program.

The Situation

Group therapy did not appear to be very helpful. Patients would make excuses, denying their problems or blaming others, and most interns would generally accept the excuses. The group members supported each other's denials as well as accepted the excuses. In each session, the patients would explore their problems, verbalize great insights, and promise not to abuse alcohol or drugs again. However, a week or two later, many of them would have fallen off the wagon again.

After I attended two sessions, I could see a mutually accepted distortion in the group's interaction as everyone in the group accepted each other's negative behavior instead of confronting it. At this time, acceptance of alcoholics' victimization was seen by some therapists as the way to help, but in practice, this reinforced the patients' bad habits.

The Program

After I experienced those first two sessions, it hit me that exercise might be a key. After all, the group had not had an intern who had been a paratrooper with the 82nd Airborne! I had the group meet me in the hospital gym for the next session. They grumbled, but eventually they all participated in an exercise class I ran that was similar to the U.S. Army's daily dozen (calisthenics). Each session, I gave each patient an opportunity to lead an exercise. I encouraged the patients during the class and confronted them when they slacked off.

After a half-hour of exercise, I held a group therapy session in the gym. We would begin by talking about their reactions to the day's exercise class, then move on to personal matters. The program continued for eight weeks, with one or two sessions a week.

The Results

Only clinical and informal conclusions can be made, since this was not a formal program implementation nor a research study. Moreover, no fitness assessments were taken to evaluate fitness changes, nor were formal assessments made in any other area. However, the following subjective conclusions can be made:

- The mere act of movement seemed to give an energy burst to the patients that was not seen in the usual group therapy session. They became active instead of passive participants in the group sessions.

- Interactions following exercise appeared more honest, reducing game-playing and distortion.
- The fitness program appeared to stimulate patients' interest in other areas, such as job training and career counseling. Rather than focusing only on "the problem" (substance abuse), they initiated inquiries into vocational areas.

Another interesting result came from an organizational standpoint. The administration of the psychology service of the hospital was rather upset about my unorthodox way of dealing with patients, asserting that physical exercise did not have a place in group therapy. Following the initial sequence of the physical training program, the decision was made to only provide traditional group therapy for the alcohol rehabilitation program.

The Learning

The following learning emerged from this experience:

- Physical training has the effect of making participants accept a more active, instead of passive, role in their situation.
- Physical training facilitates meaningful interaction. Talk alone does not necessarily produce behavior changes.
- Engaging in physical activity can lead to engaging in other important life tasks.
- Physical training can be a means to an end beyond the physical health benefits.
- Applying physical training programs for mental health or behavioral change purposes is controversial and goes against the grain of traditional therapy. You must be prepared for possible opposition to such a program.

Although tested with adults and rather loosely designed, this physical training program application made the first impression on me as to the potential of physical training programs providing one key to dealing with mental health problems.

YMCA Weight-Loss Class

My first attempt to systematically focus a physical training program on a mental health or behavioral objective was a weight control program I delivered while a YMCA director at the Golden Triangle YMCA in Pittsburgh, Pennsylvania. We offered a special class during the summer for overweight teenagers. Five male youth aged 13 to 16 enrolled in the class.

The Situation

The participants were very sedentary youth with little, if any, experience in athletics. As a consequence, they found physical training very intimidating. They appeared to be very self-conscious about their appearances, which seemed to increase their overeating and, thus, their weights.

The Program

The class met five days a week for four weeks for two and a half hours. The exercise component of the class consisted of my leading continuous rhythmic activities such as walking, jogging, calisthenics, and a pool workout (swimming, pool jogging, and bobbing). I also included a 15-minute lecture and discussion period that focused on eating and exercise habits.

The Results

This time, data were collected before and after the program to evaluate the impact of the program. The conclusions from two research studies are as follows (2, 24):

- A significant improvement in cardiovascular endurance and muscular endurance occurred.
- Associated with improvement in fitness were significant increases in positive self-concept and body image. A direct link between more positive views of their bodies (body image) and more positive perceptions of themselves (self-concept) was clear. The youth not only viewed themselves in a more positive light but also perceived themselves as being more like their ideal images of themselves.
- Also associated with improvement in fitness were significant decreases in weight and waist girth.

The significance of these results was that improving fitness had an impact on certain psychological factors (self-concept and body image) that, of course, have a bearing on mental health. Likewise, there was a relationship between improving fitness and a specific behavior change outcome, that of weight loss.

The Learning

The following learning emerged from this experience:

- To focus the physical training process on another purpose, such as improved self-concept, the leader must constantly provide encouragement and reinforcement through leading the exercise class.
- For individuals with low self-esteem, even small improvements can mean significant changes in how they view themselves. Thus, you must structure the physical activity to ensure successive and incremental gains in performance. In other words, build on successes—no matter how small!
- Group continuous rhythmical exercise increases participation.

This application documented how systematic physical training can significantly affect an individual's perception of himself and, as a consequence, how physical activity can be directly used for other physical health (e.g., obesity) and mental health purposes.

The Arkansas Rehabilitation Personal Adjustment Training Program

The Arkansas Rehabilitation Research and Training Center is a federally funded institute charged with developing innovative rehabilitation techniques for clients with physical, psychological, and social disabilities. While a senior research scientist at the center, I designed and delivered a pilot physical fitness program for use with disadvantaged and emotionally disturbed clients at a state-run rehabilitation facility.

The physical training program was incorporated into a personal adjustment training (PAT) program, which was designed to teach clients the psycho-social skills necessary to compete in the work site. The clients receiving the service were young male adults (17 to 25) in the residential rehabilitation facility. In the first two years, approximately 100 clients participated in the program, many of whom had a history of behavior problems within the rehabilitation institution.

The Situation

Because the rehabilitation clients who participated in the program were extremely unfit and appeared very disorganized and passive in how they approached activity, they needed extensive structure. I emphasized exercise leadership to provide the needed structure and enthusiasm to get them involved. Eventually, the enthusiasm caught on, and the clients became very motivated to participate, which appeared to provide a stimulus for generating a more active approach to their rehabilitation training.

Because the physical training program was both a client service and research project within the research and training center, clients were randomly assigned to the fitness program as part of their total rehabilitation plan. In addition, two control samples were selected consisting of similar clients receiving either counseling or recreational programming but not physical training.

The Program

The program consisted of a one-hour exercise session daily for a four-week period. I led a structured exercise class of continuous rhythmical activities, including aerobic training (jogging and sprints), stretching, and strength exercises (calisthenics). The workout program was structured so that progressive demands were placed on the clients to lead to improved performances (e.g., increased running distance, greater number of calisthenic repetitions, and the like). During each exercise session a 5- to 10-minute lecture period was held on fitness topics, such as exercise, nutrition, and stress management. We also discussed their relationships to the rehabilitation program. I was required to provide constant verbal feedback, encouragement, and reinforcement throughout the duration of the classes.

The Results

Since the physical training program was a research demonstration project, pretest and posttest data were collected to determine the impact of the program, including comparisons to the control samples. The conclusions from those research data are as follows (see 3, 6, 7, and 19 for details):

- Significant improvement in cardiovascular endurance and muscular endurance occurred. The control groups did not demonstrate any changes.
- Associated with an improvement in fitness were significant increases in positive self-concept and body image. The control groups did not demonstrate any changes.
- The participating clients demonstrated significant improvement in rehabilitation counselors' ratings of behavior problems and physical, emotional, and intellectual functioning compared to the control groups.
- The participating clients also demonstrated significant improvement in vocational teachers' ratings of classroom behavior and performance compared to the control groups.

The significance of these results is that a transfer of the positive fitness gains to the clients' gains in functioning within the total rehabilitation program occurred. The physical training program served as a catalyst to propel the main thrust of the rehabilitation plan: vocational training and a reduction in behavior problems. As a result, the rehabilitation center incorporated the physical training program into its personal adjustment training service area, and staff were trained to maintain the program.

The Learning

The following learning emerged from this experience:

- A structured physical training program, instead of a leisure time approach to activity, has the best probability of success for increasing fitness.

- A structured physical training program requires active exercise leadership to provide a role model and consistent reinforcement for participant performance.

- The impact of fitness gains on how you feel about yourself physically (body image) or in total (self-concept) serves as a catalyst for other behavior changes.

- The process of participating in a structured group exercise class with individual and group responsibilities can impact an individual's sense of responsibility in other areas, such as rehabilitation treatment.

- Being able to generalize the results of the physical training program to the ultimate program objective (in this case, vocational rehabilitation) makes a program acceptable. Fitness as an objective in its own right is a very low priority in this context and fitness programs will only be accepted if that link to the ultimate objective is made.

This application made the first impression on me as to how systematic physical training can significantly contribute to an individual's total rehabilitation or educational program.

Operation Survival: Camp Challenge

While at the Arkansas Rehabilitation Research and Training Center, I had the opportunity to deliver a unique survival camping program to delinquent and emotionally disturbed youth. The idea for the program grew out of my military experiences and an Outward Bound wilderness survival course I had attended. A core element of the program was physical training preparation for program participation.

The Arkansas Rehabilitation Service was receiving an increased number of teenage delinquents from juvenile probation departments and the state juvenile training schools (youth correctional agencies). The service was expected to prepare the youth to participate in existing vocational rehabilitation programs and then provide the vocational training services.

The Situation

As you might expect, most of the targeted youth were ill-prepared to participate in rehabilitation programs. As a consequence, the rehabilitation service was looking for new avenues for preparing the youth. To help meet this need, I designed a three-week survival camping program as a pilot project. The youth, aged 15 to 18, all had criminal histories of either relatively minor offenses (e.g., runaway) to more serious crimes (e.g., drug offenses and felonies). All but 1 of the 20 boys completed the program.

The group included two basic types of youth. The majority appeared to have many personal and interpersonal deficits. Their expressions of problem behaviors seemed to be attempts to overcome these deficits and belong to a group. They would go along with a strong leader—for better or worse. For them, the camp experience offered an opportunity to develop some strengths and confidence.

The other group represented boys with many strengths, which they knew how to use for their own benefit. They tended to make a game of everything during the camp experience. For them, the camp experience offered an alternative way to apply their skills.

The Program

First, the youth were divided into four teams. Each team consisted of a team leader and five boys. The team leaders were professional camp counselors who had received a week-long course training them in survival, fitness, and interpersonal skills. Then, the survival camping program was implemented in four phases.

- **Phase 1:** This consisted of one week at a residential camp. I provided basic training for survival skills, such as map and compass reading, water and food procurement, first aid, building shelters, and so on. I also led two one-hour physical training sessions a day, consisting of running and calisthenics. A major focus of this phase was to force the youths to work as a unit.
- **Phase 2:** For this phase, the group took a nine-day backpacking expedition in the Ozark Mountains. Each team had the autonomy to chart its own route as long as they maintained only a one-hour

march between teams. I had to move among all four teams on a daily basis. They carried everything they needed to survive on their backs. Over half their food had to be secured from the land (fish, wild berries, crayfish, snakes, burdock and other plants, sassafras roots, and water).

- **Phase 3:** This was a two-day debriefing period of equipment cleanup, recreation, and group and individual counseling. The focus of the discussions was on what they had learned from the experience, what they could apply to their problems or situations, and what their future vocational or school plans were now. Each participant was required to clearly define a first step of a plan for the future.

- **Phase 4:** During this time, the youth reported back to their rehabilitation counselors for follow-up planning in regard to their career programs.

Because of the nature of the camping program, teamwork was essential. Every participant had responsibilities to meet for himself and the group. For example, how well the youth got into shape during the training phase affected his and, consequently, his group's backpacking pace. How well a youth learned to read a map affected whether his group would get lost or not. The situation itself demanded cooperation and the meeting of obligations 24 hours a day or a youth would not have food, shelter, water, or fire.

Besides the physical demands of the program, the day-to-day demands of keeping the group on course and functioning required intense supervision and vigilance. At first, the boys tested all authority, but as the days progressed and the demands for day-to-day survival became clear, more trusting relationships emerged. The functional challenges of finding food and water and maintaining direction while feeling fatigued, lonely, and scared set the stage for behavior changes. Dangerous challenges arose as well, such as encounters with poisonous snakes and black bears. These aspects of the program as well as the unfamiliar surroundings served to confront the youth in an entirely different fashion than their past rehabilitation experiences had.

The Results

Because this was a research and demonstration project, several categories of pretest and posttest data were collected to evaluate the program. A few anecdotal results were so dramatic, however, they need to be mentioned.

Prior to the camping experience, one of the boys was very skinny, did not interact with others, and was afraid to try anything new. During the backpacking phase, he became more and more verbal and began to try some risky endeavors, such as being the first to go into a bat cave. Following the program, he would tense his biceps, claiming he had gained two inches. Nothing could be further from the truth for we all lost considerable weight from the experience. The important thing was that he thought he had.

Another boy was a natural leader but bounced around prior to the program, dropping out of school, and did not have any sense of direction. Following the program he went back to school and worked as a camp counselor in the summers while going to college. Several years later, I was privileged to give him a recommendation for entrance into Navy flight school.

While those are anecdotal examples of the program results, we did perform a more detailed data analysis. The following conclusions can be drawn, based on the complete data from the project (see references 4 and 5 for details):

- The participants demonstrated significant gains in cardiovascular endurance, abdominal and upper body strength, and speed.
- Associated with the fitness gains were significant increases in positive self-concept and body image.
- Also associated with the fitness gains was an increase in internal as opposed to external locus of control. This meant that the participants viewed themselves as having more control over their lives.
- Ratings by the participants' rehabilitation counselors indicated increased physical, emotional, and intellectual functioning after the camping program as well as reduced behavior problems, including increased cooperation, acceptance of responsibility, honesty, and emotional control.
- Three months following the camp program, 89% of the participating youth were in a school, job, or vocational training program, compared to a 21% figure for the group before the program.

The Camp Challenge program demonstrated that such a program could prepare youth for the more intense rehabilitation services they needed. Even with these results, the Arkansas Rehabilitation Service was not able to implement or sustain such a program, mainly due to cost. The Camp Challenge program was implemented at a cost of approximately $750 per youth. At that time, such a cost was prohibitive.

The Learning

The following learnings evolved from this experience:

- Physical fitness is a prerequisite for successfully completing any type of challenging camping program.
- The unique source of gain from a survival camp experience is that it is an uprooting experience, requiring participants to find new behaviors that relate to cooperation and responsibility.
- You must plan for specific behavioral changes. Assuming an experience will have an effect by "osmosis" is folly.
- Leadership is a critical factor. Peer leadership emerged as an important element that can be a positive force if structured and channeled.
- A physical fitness or survival camping program is only of value if it is integrated with an ongoing intervention program. Such a fitness program can serve as a "readiness" program for further involvement in behavior change programs.
- In terms of evaluation it is often difficult to separate the effects of physical training alone from the other components of the program.

This application reinforced the belief that systematic physical training must be directly linked with other services to maximize its effect as a readiness intervention.

The Dallas Police Youth Services Program

In the early 1970s, a Dallas police officer was playing Russian roulette with a juvenile he had taken into custody, and he accidentally killed the youth. Because of that incident and the attention it brought to the need for programs to serve juvenile offenders, the Dallas Police Department secured federal funds to establish a unique youth diversion program within the department. Funding was made available for a three-year period to provide services directly from the police department. Thus, the department established a unit of 12 counselors within the youth section of the criminal investigation division. I was employed to develop and direct the program, known as the Youth Services Program (YSP).

The Situation

The purpose of the program was to provide programs and services to juvenile offenders the first few times they were arrested to keep them from becoming chronic repeat offenders. Such a program had never been tried within a police department setting. As it turned out, I found that a police department is a preferable setting in which to deliver such services. Because of the uniqueness of that situation, we'll look at the nature of the staff and the youth in more detail.

Staff Selection and Training. Having had experience in law enforcement, I knew the initial challenge was to have the right staff to serve the youth, people who would fit into the police setting. If the staff did not fit in, the officers would not support the program, and eventually the services would not be effective. Before we ever served a single juvenile offender, we undertook a three-month selection and training process to mold the YSP unit.

We selected 12 counselors from over 75 applicants. For three reasons, physical fitness was a major selection criterion. First, they had to serve as role models for the youth. Second, they needed extensive energy to meet the demands of the job, which often included a 72-hour work week. Finally, they needed to have a fit image to gain initial acceptance within the department. Eight males and four females passed all the hiring standards, including a full background investigation and polygraph.

I implemented an eight-week training "academy" to not only train the counselors as to their duties but also to indoctrinate them into the police setting. During that training period, I led a daily one-hour physical training (PT) session. The group PT helped build team spirit as well as taught them to set up and run exercise classes for youth. By the time the group was ready to serve the youth, they were a lean team. We immediately put ourselves to the test by entering as a team in the department's fast pitch softball league. We won the championship, which went a long way toward our gaining acceptance within the department.

Program Participants. Having met the first demand of preparing a well-trained and energetic staff, we soon took on the real challenge of influencing the young offenders. Fortunately, the Texas Youth Council had commissioned a study of the youthful offenders in the state, defining areas for which services were needed. That report showed that the youth who were arrested lacked many physical, emotional, and intellectual skills as well as the discipline and structure in their lives to learn those skills. The findings helped us define what we should provide through the YSP program.

Whether from a rich or impoverished background, the youth had the same problems. They lacked structure and adult supervision in their lives. The majority of them had little or no responsibility or accountability. At home, in school, and on the street, they seemed to bounce around with little or no direction. This was especially a problem during free time. Neither did they have any goals or concept of self-discipline.

A few youth used their intelligence to be better criminals; they were the leaders. The majority, however, seemed to get in trouble because they didn't pay attention to what the consequences of their behavior would or could be. Add to that very little constructive direction from family or friends and it was not surprising to see the juvenile arrest statistics.

The youth approached the program with a "wait and see" attitude. Because of the police-based nature of the program, very little disruptive behavior occurred. They felt they had to be at the sessions because the sessions were provided by the police, although participation was not mandated by the court. Consequently, they functioned as a captive audience. As time went on, the youths became more active, participating fully in activities and discussions. The physical training sessions were critical to getting them to interact and discuss their behavior and its consequences.

Over the course of the first three years (during which there was a formal program evaluation), approximately 3000 juvenile offenders, ranging from 13 to 17 years, were served by the program—10% of all youth arrests in Dallas at that time. Although originally intended to serve the first time minor offender, the offense breakdown of the youth indicated approximately 45% were felony offenders and approximately 30% were repeat offenders. Certainly, the program served more than merely the "Mickey Mouse" offender.

The Program

The YSP program contained many elements of which the physical training sessions were only one component. After being arrested, the youth and his parents signed a behavioral contract to participate in the YSP for six months. Although not a legal document, the act of signing the contract encouraged participation.

Besides the direct services provided by the YSP within the police department, an additional support program was also developed using Dallas firefighters. A 16-hour training session was provided to selected Dallas firefighters from each fire station, that taught them how to function as firefighter counselors to the youth. Each youth was assigned to a firefighter counselor at a fire station near her home as a follow-up program. The firefighter normally worked with the youth on a recreation or hobby area and then supervised the YSP follow-up program.

The entire program was designed in a systematic manner, including written procedures, curriculum, lesson plans, and youth and parent workbook materials. The program consisted of three phases.

- **Phase 1 (intake):** This phase involved assessing each youth's fitness level; interpersonal skills; study skills; and problems within home, school, and free time settings. We usually conducted this assessment in one meeting at the youth's home or at the police station.

- **Phase 2 (direct):** This consisted of one three-hour weekly meeting for four weeks. At each meeting the youth experienced a module on physical fitness, including 30 to 45 minutes of physical training, a module on interpersonal skills, a module on study skills, and discussion of their responsibilities. Following the completion of the direct phase, we assessed the youth in a way similar to the intake phase. Associated with the youth sessions were at least one parent session in which the parents were taught behavior contracting with their child. Then we assigned the parents the responsibility of using the behavior contracts to ensure youth participation in the direct and follow-up program phases.

- **Phase 3 (follow-up):** The third phase consisted of one meeting a month for four months. We assigned each youth to a follow-up program in each of three areas: fitness and recreation, home responsibilities, and school responsibilities. The majority of youth were also assigned to a firefighter counselor for ongoing follow-up programming.

The physical training component of the direct program phase consisted of both activity and education on how to maintain a program. Physical fitness was presented as a skill, not simply as a process. The youth learned to set fitness goals and design an exercise plan. Each exercise class consisted of jogging, calisthenics, and stretching activities. The youths then worked through a "Getting Fit" workbook, which outlined a fitness program to maintain at home. Then prior to the follow-up phase, we gave the youths a "Getting Active" workbook, which led them through a brief module on how to select a recreation or sport activity. The YSP counselors then asked each youth to enroll in a structured recreation or sport program in his neighborhood. We allowed youths to choose to stay with a home fitness activity, join a recreation program, or do both.

The Results

Many areas warrant discussion. The first area is the effectiveness of providing the program within a police setting. As with other physical training applications, the YSP program was very controversial. The mental health community expressed the concern that a police department is not the place to provide services to youth. Likewise, concern was expressed within the department that it was not the job of police to do "social work."

As it turned out, a police department was the ideal setting because youthful offenders need authority figures. One of the problems in many social service programs with at-risk youth is the lack of authority and discipline within those settings. A police department can provide the authority for behavior changes to occur.

From an anecdotal perspective, hundreds of youth and parents expressed gratitude for the Dallas Police Department's initiative. For example, a single parent welfare mother who had two boys assigned to the program reported that after she applied the behavior contract training with her boys she for the first time saw a way to direct and control her boys. She was not alone! Many of the youth were simply out of control, and the program provided the means by which parents and the youth themselves could assume control.

The bottom line for any program is the effect the program has on doing what it is intended to do. As a federally funded project, it had a very strong evaluation component in the program. Data collected before and after the program were analyzed on the first 887 participants to complete the YSP. A control sample of 253 youth who met the criteria for the program but did not participate provided comparison data. The conclusions of the reported data are as follows (see references 16, 17, 18, 25, 26, 27, and 28 for more details):

- The participating youth demonstrated increased fitness (cardio-vascular endurance, strength, and flexibility) as well as increased emotional and intellectual skills.

- Associated with the skill gains were increased responsible behaviors in home, school, and leisure settings. For example, the youth demonstrated a 54% increase in doing chores at home, a 60% decrease in school discipline problems, and a 49% increase in participation in structured recreation programs.

- The youth who completed the YSP had a significantly lower recidivism rate than the control sample or the total juvenile rearrest rate for Dallas. For an 18-month period, the YSP youth had a 10.6% rearrest rate, the control sample had a 42.7% rate, and the total rearrest rate was 53.3%.

- Those YSP youth who did recidivate had significantly fewer repeat offenses and repeat felony offenses than the control sample.

- During the reporting period for the data analysis, the total recidivism for all Dallas youth, the total referrals to the juvenile court, and the total juvenile court hearings rates were significantly reduced.

- The YSP was recognized as the exemplary juvenile diversion program in Texas.

The federal funding for the YSP was depleted after three years of operation. In response to the demonstrated effectiveness of the program, the Dallas Police Department budgeted tax revenue to fund the YSP program on a sustaining basis as part of the department's normal operational budget. As a consequence, the YSP has been in existence within the Dallas Police Department for over 20 years. It is one of few federally sponsored programs that a municipality has funded after the federal funds were expended.

The Learning

The following learning emerged from this experience:

- The leadership component again was highlighted as the key to program success. Carefully selecting and adequately training staff was very important.
- Contrary to popular perceptions, at-risk youth want and are seeking a positive source of structure and discipline.
- When the youths' deficits are control and structure, the physical training program can be a natural vehicle to assist them in gaining control and structure in their lives.
- For the physical training program to meet a variety of objectives, it must be systematically developed to meet those objectives. A well-planned curriculum ensures systematic, instead of random, learning.
- Teaching youth how to design a physical fitness program also teaches them goal setting and planning skills.
- If the physical training activity can be transferred to other activities such as sports and structured recreation, the probability of fitness maintenance is maximized. Every minute a youth is involved in recreational activity is one minute she cannot be getting into trouble.
- For youth who are out of control, a structured situation that focuses on disciplined learning may be more important than the content of the curriculum. The physical domain offers that concrete, disciplined learning context.
- Involving parents in the process increases the probability of sustaining the fitness and other behavioral changes.
- If the ultimate objective (in this case, it was reducing recidivism) is reached through physical training, others will accept and institutionalize the program.

This application documented that if the physical training program is the main element, rather than just an ancillary element of a larger effort with a larger objective, its impact can be capitalized upon. Moreover, this application proved that you can train social service and criminal justice personnel to provide physical training programming.

The First Choice Program

The "War on Drugs" in the 1980s and 1990s focused attention on the need to develop innovative strategies to deal with the problem of substance abuse. In response, I designed a structured physical training program called "First Choice" to reduce substance abuse habits among at-risk youth in community- and school-based prevention and rehabilitation settings. Since its initiation, the First Choice program has been installed in over 50 sites in several states through a series of grants for substance abuse prevention. While the objective of most installations was substance abuse prevention, at most sites the program has evolved into a focused inner city neighborhood physical fitness program. In many instances, a community or organization would not support a physical training program simply to increase fitness, but when it was promoted as a tool to prevent drug abuse, the support became very strong.

Based upon previous experience in applying physical training programs, I defined a curriculum aimed at substance abuse and violence prevention, using physical training that could be replicated in a variety of settings. I designed a "train the trainer" installation model to empower recreation and prevention program staff, schoolteachers, institutional staff, and inner city youth service staff to implement the program. The First Choice program represents the latest and most-defined application of physical training programming for at-risk youth, so a more lengthy discussion of it is presented here.

The Situation

The First Choice program was initially applied in the Dallas–Fort Worth area. The program was installed in 10 sites, including a school district alternative high school, a substance abuse counseling agency, the Dallas County Juvenile Probation Department, a residential treatment hospital, and several metropolitan inner city YMCAs. Additional installations have been made in school-based programs in Washington, DC and Charlotte, North Carolina.

The largest installation is in the state of Illinois. The Illinois Department of Alcohol and Substance Abuse (DASA) with support of the Illinois Governor's Council on Physical Fitness and Sports, has funded several installations throughout the state. Specifically, I have installed

First Choice programs in over 30 prevention and treatment sites throughout the state over a six-year period, including school sites, residential treatment centers, inner city YMCAs, inner city recreation centers, juvenile correctional institutions, housing development service agencies such as the Boys and Girls Clubs, community mental health and public health centers, and National Guard armory settings. Most recently, we have used First Choice as citizenship development and gang prevention interventions for Laotian and Bosnian refugee relocation programs. My focus in all installation efforts has been on training staff and providing curriculum to implement the First Choice program.

While the funding sources for these installations were from substance abuse funding agencies, the majority of youth served did not have any illicit drug behaviors prior to the program, making the sites delivering the program mainly prevention programs. Some youths served, however, are incarcerated drug users and pushers. Others live in housing projects or rural communities and participate in neighborhood recreation centers or after-school programs. As can be seen, such a physical training program is applicable for helping youth at all risk levels.

The initial installations provided feedback that helped us focus the First Choice program to better meet the needs of the youth. I found that we had to make three major alterations or extensions of the basic program.

First was the recognition that the closer each First Choice site could be to the neighborhood of the youth the program served, the greater the participation. As a consequence, later installations were aimed at neighborhood-based programs directly in or near high population areas such as housing projects.

A second major change occurred when other services were added to support the basic physical training program for youth. Neighborhood physical fitness councils and a peer fitness leader program called FITCORPS were used to support the implementation of First Choice.

The third extension to the program was the acknowledgment that a need existed for ongoing support and training for the fitness leaders and peer leaders in each neighborhood. Along with that need was the need for a coordinating organization that could provide the First Choice program directly to youth. As a consequence, I obtained additional funding to implement a master trainer program to train selected members of the Illinois National Guard to provide ongoing training and supervision in neighborhoods on a sustaining basis. The Guard was selected because of its strong commitment to the communities it serves and because it was a logical extension of the Guard's drug demand reduction mission.

As are all state Guards, the Illinois National Guard is charged with a counter drug and demand reduction mission, leading to more site opportunities for First Choice. The Illinois Guard adopted the First Choice program as its drug demand reduction initiative and implemented the program in five Guard armory sites across the state, providing the physical fitness program directly to youth in communities adjacent to armories. These armory sites serve as community fitness centers for the youth. Youth volunteer to participate as they would in a city recreation program. In this way, the Guard initiative serves as a primary program for preventing substance abuse.

The experience of applying First Choice within community-based agencies, especially those in the inner city, has led me to take a unique perspective on such situations. Specifically, we can draw some conclusions as to the nature of the youths, the helping staffs serving the youth, and the organizations those staff work for that can help us better understand the uniqueness of these installation situations.

The Youth. It became very clear from the delivery of the first installation of the First Choice program that the issue was not a specific substance abuse or any other disruptive behavior. They were but symptoms of a dysfunctional lifestyle.

The majority of youth (especially those in the inner city) had many deficits. They had a history of poor school performance, poor school attendance, poor social relationships or negative relationships such as gang membership, and little, if any, participation in sports. They also were not very physically fit nor had any well-developed motor skills.

Like the youth served in the other fitness programs described, they had very little, if any, structure in their lives. Parental or adult authority was almost nonexistent, leading to an extension of the deficits. The value system surrounding their lives appeared to be one of expediency and selfishness. No concept of community or of positive community values to offset the street values existed. The words of one of the "saints" who has been working with youth in a Chicago housing development for decades illustrates the challenge of working in the inner city. The Major, as he was called, had served in a Boys Club in a large sprawling housing development for over 40 years. Seventy-five percent of the youth were from single parent families and the majority of parents were drug users. When I asked how he stayed optimistic, he replied, "If you want to try to change things in the housing project or the neighborhood—forget it. You have to think of affecting one kid at a time. It is the only way."

Staff Serving the Youth. There is no question that the majority of staff serving at-risk youth—especially in the inner city—are dedicated to the cause. Yet I discovered that many were so overwhelmed and undertrained that the necessary program structure was many times simply not there. Even the highest trained teaching and social work staff demonstrated, at times, very little structure and discipline in their efforts. For some, the fitness leader training program was the first structured and accountable training they had received for working in their respective youth programs.

A minority of staff we trained to implement the First Choice program reflected behavior of the youth they were serving. Probably the most apparent similar behavior was the absence of responsibility skills, such as arriving for meetings on time, completing assignments, and following directions. In many respects, I had to structure the fitness leader programs in a similar fashion to army training to ensure trainees were accountable. This problem was one reason for the recruitment of the National Guard to play a key role in the community-based programs.

Emphasis was always placed on leadership. While the program is important, it was the leader who gets out on the gym floor and playground that makes the critical difference.

Fortunately, the majority of the staff were able to master the content of training and apply the First Choice program to their settings, successfully integrating the First Choice program and making the unique modifications that their settings dictated. They did an outstanding job—often with limited resources and support.

Organizations Serving the Youth. Most community-based organizations serving at-risk youth operate on limited funds. Often, organizations must rely on volunteers to maintain services. Likewise, these organizations often lose their short-term funding and suspend services, then reemerge later.

As with the helping staff, the leadership of many of the organizations lacked the management training to supervise and oversee a service organization. Many organizations did not have any accountability built into their operations. Many of the community-based programs had a very loosely organized and haphazard approach to delivering services. Yet, it was amazing how some of the administrators were able to sustain an organization with limited funds, staff, and resources. But many did, which reflects the grass roots commitment by many to help their youth as best as they can.

The Program

Three major aspects of the program need to be examined: (1) the components of the First Choice fitness program that the youth received, (2) the preparation for installation, and (3) the leadership training of staff to implement the program.

Program Components. I provided a formal curriculum consisting of lesson plans and manuals to trained staff to initiate the program at each site. The First Choice program had five major elements.

1. **Educational and physical activity classes:** As with some earlier applications, these classes taught fitness as a life skill. We used group exercise classes focusing on running, stretching, calisthenics, and weight training to increase fitness. The educational components focused on teaching assessment, goal setting, and exercise planning as life skills. The youth worked through a manual to develop a personalized fitness program. Leaders also held discussion sessions to explore the youths' behaviors, values, and feelings regarding fitness and exercise, substance abuse, and other destructive behavior. Throughout the activity and educational sessions, the program focused on the values of respect, responsibility, and self-discipline. Besides the physical fitness and exercise content, the educational component also focused on other health promotion topics, such as nutrition and stress management. At some sites additional modules were offered, covering how maintaining a fit lifestyle could prevent substance abuse and violence.

2. **Parent support training:** The training was intended to increase family activity participation. Content focused on behavior contracting, family fitness activities, and personal walking programs.

3. **A peer fitness leader training program:** This program was to teach community service. Selected youth were trained to participate in the First Choice FITCORPS. They helped implement fitness classes and special events and assisted with equipment maintenance and younger participants in the program. An extension of that program involved a career exploration and internship program for the fitness and recreation fields.

4. **Physical fitness councils:** These neighborhood councils ensured ongoing support and expanded activity programming. They were implemented only in the neighborhood fitness sites in the city of Chicago.

5. **Existing community resources:** First Choice facilitated the coordination and use of community resources, including special events to serve youth fitness and sport activity needs.

Program Preparation. Prior to implementing the First Choice program at a given site, a considerable number of planning meetings were necessary. For the program to succeed, each site had to assume ownership of the program. Specifically, participating sites had to commit to four responsibilities as conditions of participation, including

- delivering the program for one year,
- dedicating staff and resources to provide the program,
- assigning staff to receive the fitness leadership training, and
- collecting program evaluation data.

I conducted many preparation meetings to formalize how the First Choice program would fit within existing services. The program would only succeed if it were accepted and readily incorporated into day-to-day operations. Each site's program was configured to fit within its unique service structure. Example configurations include the following:

- Inner city and community agency settings (recreation centers, YMCAs, National Guard armories, and substance abuse and mental health counseling centers) would have a 12-week program meeting three days a week. Several sites also offered the program as a summer day camp program.
- Residential treatment centers, correctional institutions, and juvenile justice settings would offer First Choice on a daily basis in repeating 12- to 16-week cycles.
- School-based sites would offer First Choice as either a semester-long physical education course or as an after-school program meeting, usually three days a week.

Leadership Training. Implementation of the First Choice program was based on the premise that leadership was the key element. As a consequence, I developed and implemented a "train the trainer" program and curriculum installation process to empower the neighborhood or community to provide the program on a sustaining basis.

The on-site neighborhood fitness leaders were a combination of parents, local fitness staff (YMCAs, park districts, Boys Clubs, and the like), and community volunteers. The school and residential treatment center staff were professional teachers and social workers and counselors.

The basic fitness leader program consisted of a one-week, 40-hour course, after which trainees had to pass both a written and practical examination to be certified as fitness leaders. To ensure consistent and systematic program delivery, we gave each trainee a curriculum consisting of lesson plans divided into modules and participant handbooks. The module approach allowed trainees to configure the program elements to fit within their organizational structures. Over 250 fitness leaders have been trained through 18 courses.

A master trainer training program was established to train community fitness leaders so that they would have the level of expertise to train additional neighborhood fitness leaders and expand installation sites. To this end, I designed another 40-hour training course and delivered it to selected master trainers. Master trainer programs were delivered in Charlotte, North Carolina and in Illinois using the National Guard.

In addition to the master trainer training a follow-up training, monitoring, and support system was implemented with the help of existing resources such as the National Guard.

The Results

Two areas of results are especially worthy of examination. The first area pertains to the impact of the First Choice program on participating youth and the second pertains to the training model for installing the program.

Impact on Youth. So far, over 4000 youth have participated in the First Choice program. The program has had an extensive evaluation component in all settings to assess the validity of the program as a fitness program and as a substance abuse prevention intervention. The major research conclusions are as follows (see references 8 through 15 and 20 through 23 for more details):

- Participating youth significantly increased their levels of activity and fitness (cardiovascular endurance, strength, and flexibility).
- Associated with improvements in fitness was alleviation of several substance abuse risk factors. For example, a significant increase in rated self-concept and a significant decrease in anxiety, depression, and school-related problems occurred.
- We gave a self-report substance abuse inventory to approximately 600 of the participating youth before and after participating in the program. The results indicated significant reductions in the use of cigarettes, smokeless tobacco, inhalants, alcohol, marijuana, cocaine, hallucinogens, uppers, and steroids. Concurrently, a significant reduction in multiple drug use and a significant increase in total abstinence occurred.
- In evaluating the program, the youth themselves rated it highly valuable.
- Both parents and community agency personnel working with the First Choice program rated it as a valuable and necessary service within the community.
- The program was recognized at the National Youth Fitness Summit as one of the 20 exemplary youth fitness programs in the nation and was recommended by the American College of Sports Medi-

cine as one of four programs that should be disseminated nationally to meet the *Healthy People 2000* goals (1, 29).

The real significance of these results was characterized by the fact that the Illinois Department of Alcohol and Substance Abuse made an ongoing commitment to expand the First Choice program by providing continuous funding to install First Choice in communities throughout the state.

Effectiveness of Program Installation. We can make the following conclusions about the effectiveness of the training installation process:

- The training program to train organizational staff serving youth in regard to the First Choice fitness program skills was effective. Of those staff trained, 82% met the certification criteria by passing both written and practical examinations.
- Of those organizations that sent staff to training, 85% were able to successfully implement First Choice as intended. The major reason given by organizations for not implementing First Choice was a budget cutback or staff layoffs after the training.
- Participating sites institutionalized the program so they could sustain it on a regular basis.

In short, the installation design worked to expand the First Choice program to other sites to, in turn, impact more youth.

The Learning

The installation of the First Choice program reinforced the learning from the other applications of fitness programs. Some of the major new or reiterated learnings are as follows:

- The gains in physical fitness appear to translate directly to changes in problem behavior risk factors and actual problem behaviors such as substance abuse.
- A program must have a variety of activities, including special events, to keep youth interested. For example, providing sport tournaments and outings such as going to ball games are especially helpful.
- Many professionals in the field stated that at-risk youth would not respond to this approach. They were wrong: At-risk youth are seeking positive sources of discipline in their lives.
- The results demonstrated that it is possible to empower the neighborhood community to deliver the services.

- Once again, the importance of leadership was clear. And staff *can* be adequately trained with the skills and curriculum to initiate the physical training program successfully.
- Providing a peer fitness leader program maximizes youth involvement and aids in developing a sense of program ownership within a neighborhood or community.
- Follow-up training and technical support are needed to provide consistent backing for the neighborhood site fitness leaders. The master trainer model appears to appropriately meet that objective.
- The full benefit of the fitness intervention can only be realized if it is integrated with existing services.
- A problem of "turf" when linking with community-based services may arise. It is critical to establish relationships so that the program is viewed as an enhancement and not a competing entity.
- Program acceptance is based on evaluation results. Most programs serving at-risk youth have little, if any, evaluation data to assess their effect. Because evaluation is built in, First Choice has been sustained at the application sites on an ongoing basis.
- To be accepted and funded, physical fitness programs have to be promoted in a way in which they are seen as helpful tools for dealing with community concerns such as substance abuse.

The true test of the validity of any intervention is whether it can be duplicated and expanded. This application documented that a systematic physical training program such as First Choice can be transferred to a variety of community-based settings through a training installation model. That model enables a broader application of the program and ensures quality results.

Conclusion

The development of systematic physical training programs that can affect factors other than physical ones has been somewhat of a journey. Each form of the program helped me learn how to make the next application even better. The First Choice program represents the latest and most developed form. All applications have led to the following main conclusions:

- A chain of effect results from applying physical training. Positive changes in physical activity level and physical fitness are associated with positive changes in psycho-social risk factors, such as self-concept, depression, and school functioning. In turn, positive changes in serious problem behavior, such as substance abuse and criminality, occur.

- The chain of effect does not occur unless changes in physical activity level and physical fitness occur.
- Changes in physical activity level and physical fitness do not occur without quality leadership.
- Changes in physical activity level and physical fitness do not occur without systematic and structured physical training programs.
- The changes noted have strong data to support the value of physical training.

Through the application of physical training and fitness programs to dealing with the at-risk youth puzzle, I have strived to make the best use of physical training for the most human benefit. I look forward, however, to developing more advanced forms of physical fitness programming as we continue to learn more about how exercise can be a critical piece of the solution to the at-risk puzzle.

References

1. American College of Sports Medicine. 1996. Children and youth focus of project summary: Healthy People 2000. *Sports Medicine Bulletin* 31(3):4.
2. Collingwood, T. 1971. The effects of physical training upon body attitude and self-concept. *Discussion Papers* 10(3). Hot Springs, AR: Arkansas Rehabilitation Research and Training Center.
3. ———. 1972. Physical fitness: A process goal for rehabilitating clients. *Rehabilitation Research and Practice Review* 3(3):71-75.
4. ———. 1972. Survival camping: A therapeutic mode for rehabilitating problem youth. Monograph series. Hot Springs, AR: Arkansas Rehabilitation Research and Training Center.
5. ———. 1972. Survival camping with problem youth. *Rehabilitation Record* 1(13): 22-26.
6. ———. 1972. The effects of physical training upon behavior and self attitudes. *Journal of Clinical Psychology* 28(3):583-585.
7. ———. 1972. The effects of systematic physical, intellectual and emotional personal adjustment program. *Research Reports*, vol. 1. Hot Springs, AR: Arkansas Rehabilitation Research and Training Center.
8. ———. 1992. *An evaluation of the Fitness Intervention Training program on substance abuse prevention*. Los Angeles: The Nancy Reagan Foundation.

9. ———. 1992. *Fitness intervention training: An evaluation of the installation of physical fitness programs for substance abuse and prevention.* Springfield, IL: Illinois Department of Alcohol and Substance Abuse.

10. ———. 1992. *Fitness intervention training: Applications for neighborhood fitness programming to counteract substance abuse.* Springfield, IL: Illinois Department of Alcohol and Substance Abuse.

11. ———. 1993. *Fitness leadership development for neighborhood fitness programming to counteract substance abuse.* Springfield, IL: Illinois Department of Alcohol and Substance Abuse.

12. ———. 1994. *Neighborhood fitness programs as substance abuse prevention services.* Springfield, IL: Illinois Department of Alcohol and Substance Abuse.

13. ———. 1994. *Program evaluation: The Illinois National Guard Operation First Choice fitness program.* Springfield, IL: Illinois National Guard.

14. ———. 1996. *Program evaluation: The Illinois National Guard Operation First Choice fitness program.* Springfield, IL: Illinois National Guard.

15. ———. 1994. The application of physical fitness programming for substance abuse prevention and treatment. *Directions in Substance Abuse Counseling* 2(5):1-9.

16. Collingwood, T., A. Douds, H. Williams, and R. Wilson. 1979. *Developing youth resources.* Amherst, MA: Human Resource Development Press.

17. Collingwood, T., and M. Englesjgerd. 1977. Physical fitness, delinquency, and delinquency prevention. *Journal of Physical Education, Recreation and Dance* 48(6):23.

18. Collingwood, T., and B. Genthner. 1980. Skills training as treatment for juvenile delinquents. *Professional Psychology* 11:591-598.

19. Collingwood, T., and R. Jones. 1972. Physical training as an aid to client rehabilitation. *Discussion Papers* 13(13). Hot Springs, AR: Arkansas Rehabilitation Research and Training Center.

20. Collingwood, T., R. Reynolds, B. Jester, and D. DeBord. 1992. Enlisting physical education for the war on drugs. *Journal of Physical Education, Recreation and Dance* 63(2):25-28.

21. Collingwood, T., R. Reynolds, and H.W. Kohl. 1990. Effects of physical training on adolescent substance abuse risk factors and patterns: Abstract. *Medicine and Science in Sport and Exercise* S22(2):578.

22. Collingwood, T., R. Reynolds, H.W. Kohl, and S. Sloan. 1991. Physical fitness effects on substance abuse risk factors and use patterns: A preliminary study. *Journal of Drug Education* 21(1):73-84.

23. Collingwood, T., J. Sunderlin, and H.W. Kohl. 1994. The use of a staff training model for implementing fitness programming to prevent substance abuse with at-risk youth. *American Journal of Health Promotion* 9(1):20-23.

24. Collingwood, T., and L. Willett. 1971. The effects of physical training upon self-concept and body attitude. *Journal of Clinical Psychology* 27:411-412.

25. Collingwood, T., H. Williams, and A. Douds. 1976. An HRD approach to police diversion for juvenile offenders. *Personnel and Guidance Journal* 54(8):435-437.

26. ———. 1976. Juvenile diversion: The youth service program. *Federal Probation* 40(3):23-27.

27. Collingwood, T., and R. Wilson. 1976. Police diversion: A vehicle to prevent juvenile recidivism. *Police Chief* 43(12):38-39.

28. ———. 1976. The Dallas Police Department's youth services program. *Texas Police Journal* 23(12):16-18.

29. President's Council on Physical Fitness and Sports. 1991. *National Youth Fitness Summit.* Washington, DC: Government Printing Office.

The Structure of the Physical Training Program

Part II provides guidelines for the actual delivery of a physical training program to at-risk youth. The guidelines are based on the experience (described in part I) of 25 years of delivering physical fitness programming to at-risk youth, particularly the First Choice program. Five basic physical training program elements are described to help you organize your plans:

1. Health screening and physical fitness assessment to provide a baseline for improvement
2. Structured physical exercise classes
3. Educational classes that teach youth to assess their own fitness levels, set fitness goals, and design individual fitness programs
4. Teaching values by integrating them into the exercise and educational components
5. Support programs that aid in sustaining youths' involvement, such as peer leader opportunities and parent and community involvement programs

Each chapter in this section focuses on a different element of the program and how that element ensures that a youth proceeds successfully through the program.

Chapter 4 gives guidelines for health screening and physical fitness assessment testing, the initial program elements you need to provide in a physical training program. Specific procedures are presented with sample forms for you to use in screening.

Chapter 5 spells out the guidelines for structuring exercise so that physical activity produces a training effect. Sample group exercise routines along with guidelines for ensuring exercise safety are provided.

Chapter 6 offers guidelines for educational programming that teaches physical fitness as a life skill. The instructional guidelines cover screening, fitness assessment, profiling, goal setting, exercise planning, and self-control skill modules, and they include sample forms. Finally, guidelines for helping youth transfer fitness life skills to other areas such as substance abuse are provided.

Chapter 7 contains suggested guidelines for teaching values and managing and motivating behavior change. Strategies for using exercise activities, educational activities, and interactions and discussions with participants to teach values behaviors are presented. In addition, guidelines for using incentive plans both to teach values and to motivate participants to adopt positive values and exercise behaviors are provided.

Chapter 8 covers guidelines for integrating support programs into your basic physical training program. Several program areas are addressed, including parent programs, a peer fitness leader program, use of community resources through a physical fitness council, special events, and motivation program strategies.

Chapter 4

Physical Fitness Screening and Assessment Programming

Before youth participate in any type of physical fitness or physical training program, they must go through a screening and assessment process. Knowing an individual's health and fitness status is necessary before providing any kind of exercise activity. One of the reasons why some youth do not respond favorably to physical activity is because they are thrown into an exercise program without evaluation prior to participation. If the intensity level of the physical training program is not appropriate to the individual's current abilities, he or she may drop out because it is too easy or too hard. The screening and assessment process, the initial program elements, are there to insure the program fits each individual.

Screening

Screening is the first step in setting up an individualized program. This systematic data gathering process helps determine if exercise is safe for an individual. The purpose is not to diagnose disease or health problems but to determine the risk of exercise. While screening is not as significant an issue for youth as it is for adults, you still need to do some. The following information on screening guidelines and forms should help you do that.

Screening Guidelines

A complete screening process addresses five general areas of risk:

- Orthopedic problems
- Cardiovascular and pulmonary problems
- Psychological problems
- Medication problems
- Metabolic problems

You can obtain most of the information on the presence of these risk factors through a health history questionnaire or through a medical screening process.

You can use a simple screening levels program for screening youth for exercise participation. Figure 4.1 presents two levels. The normal progression is to have youth proceed directly from level 1 to level 2. If high risk indicators appear, have that youth undergo the health and medical examination process (levels 1A and 2A) for further screening.

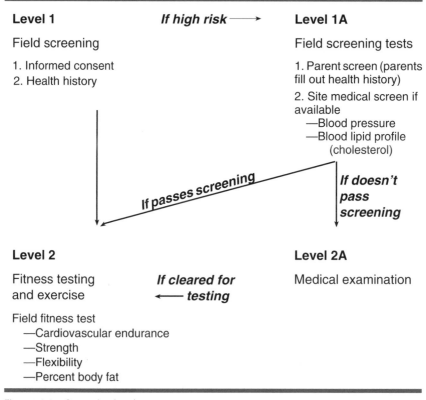

Figure 4.1   Screening levels process.

Screening Forms

Two forms can be used for health screening: an informed consent form and the health history form.

Informed Consent Form. An informed consent form is a brief document that the youth and parents read and sign. It contains information about what is involved in the exercise program, what the risks are, and what you expect of program staff and participants.

An informed consent form should be signed before a youth participates in the program. By having the youth and parent or guardian sign this form before participating, you may prevent misunderstandings should injuries or other problems occur (see figure 4.2).

Health History Form. The health history form can be used to gather background information on any major health problems or risks for a youth. Have each youth fill out this form the first day that he or she enters the physical training program to determine how he or she proceeds through the screening levels system. See figure 4.3 for an example.

Physical Fitness Assessment

Physical fitness assessment is, in a way, a continuation of screening. Through testing, you can help an individual find his or her level of physical fitness. Specifically, the fitness assessment has four purposes:

1. To assess each area of fitness so the individual can see which fitness areas require attention
2. To find a starting point for beginning an exercise program
3. To establish a baseline against for measuring improvements
4. To provide a comparison point for motivation

The recommended youth fitness battery consists of the following tests (described in detail in the appendix) that measure the basic physical fitness areas:

- Skinfold calipers to measure percent body fat
- One-minute push-up test to measure upper body muscular endurance
- One-minute sit-up test to measure abdominal muscular endurance
- Sit-and-reach test to measure flexibility
- One-mile run to measure cardiovascular endurance

Informed Consent Form
for Physical Fitness Programming

1. Introductory statement

You have chosen to participate in the physical training program. The following information explains that program. Please read it carefully and do not hesitate to ask questions about the fitness program or the information below.

2. Purpose of the program

The purpose of the program is to increase your activity and fitness level so that your physical and emotional well-being is improved.

3. Program activities

Program activities will include filling out a written health history, completing an exercise test battery, and taking part in a variety of physical exercises. The purpose of the testing is to assess physical fitness level. All testing and exercise activities will be supervised by trained fitness leaders. These activities will include running, weight and calisthenic strength exercises, stretching, and athletics. You may be expected to follow an individual program on your own time as part of the program. All records will be held in confidence. The testing data will be used in an anonymous manner to evaluate the effects of the program.

4. Discomforts and risks

Certain physical events may occur during exercise testing and exercise. These events may include heat-related illnesses, abnormal heartbeats and blood pressure, and in rare instances, injuries. Professional care in the selection and supervision of participants provides appropriate precautions against such problems but does not ensure they will not occur.

5. Questions

If you have any additional questions, please notify the staff of the physical training program.

(continued)

Figure 4.2   Sample informed consent form.

6. Authorization

I have read this form and understand that inherent risks are associated with any physical activity and recognize that it is my responsibility to provide accurate and complete health history information. To the best of my knowledge, there are no contraindications to my participation and I agree to participate.

_____   _____
Participant's signature   Date

_____   _____
Parent's or guardian's signature   Witness's signature

Figure 4.2 *(continued)*
Adapted, by permission, from *Physical fitness specialist course*, 1993 (Dallas: The Cooper Institute for Aerobics Research).

These tests have been validated for use with youth and are used in various youth fitness testing batteries across the country. Other test batteries, such as the *Fitnessgram* test of the Cooper Institute for Aerobics Research and the *Physical Best* test of the American Alliance for Health, Physical Education, Recreation and Dance, may have a few different items and norms but they all measure the same fitness areas.

To ensure a valid testing process follow these three sets of procedures:

1. Test preparation
2. Youth preparation
3. General test administration

Test Preparation

Advance preparation is always a key before administering a testing battery. It includes three tasks: scheduling the fitness assessment, organizing the test site and equipment, and attending to safety factors.

- **Task 1. Scheduling the fitness assessment.** Give participants the schedule at the first class meeting.

Health History

Directions: You and your parents need to fill out all items.

Name _____

Date _____

Age _____

Sex _____

Directions: Please check if you have any of these problems.

Yes

_____ 1. Heart disease or heart problems

_____ 2. Hypertension (high blood pressure)

_____ 3. Stroke

_____ 4. Diabetes or abnormal blood sugar test

_____ 5. Epilepsy or seizures

_____ 6. Abnormal chest X-ray

_____ 7. Asthma

_____ 8. Orthopedic or muscular problems

_____ 9. Overweight

_____ 10. Any other major health problems (If *yes*, please list below.)

_____

_____ 11. Use of prescription drugs (If *yes*, please list drugs below.)

_____

_____ 12. Do you smoke?

_____ 13. Do you have close relatives (mother, father, sister, brother) who have a history of heart disease? (If *yes*, please list names below.) _____

_____

Figure 4.3 Sample health history form.

- **Task 2. Organizing the test site and equipment.** Check to be sure all equipment is working. Set up five separate stations in the following sequence:

  1 = Skinfold
  2 = Push-ups
  3 = Sit-and-reach
  4 = Sit-ups
  5 = Mile run

  Have the youth rotate through the first four stations, allowing ample rest between each station. Then perform the mile run as a group with a full 15-minute rest period prior to the run.

- **Task 3. Attending to safety factors.** Check the weather before proceeding. If it is too hot or cold, you may want to delay testing. See chapter 5 for more on environmental factors in exercise. Also be sure to have a first aid kit and water in place before testing.

After attending to these three tasks, you are ready to prepare the youth themselves.

Youth Preparation

The two preparation tasks for youth are test briefing and physical preparation for testing.

- **Task 1. Test briefing.** Fully inform the youths about the test situation and expectations, including the following:

  — Explain the purpose of the testing.

  — Describe the symptoms of overexertion to watch for, such as dizziness, pain, or difficulty breathing. Tell them to stop exercising and walk if they experience any such symptoms.

  — Teach and demonstrate the procedures for each test. Provide feedback on proper form and technique.

- **Task 2. Physical preparation of youth.** To prepare youth for the actual testing, tell them to refrain from drinking any caffeinated beverages or eating food during the hour prior to testing. Conduct a formal warm-up session prior to initiating testing with ballistic movements such as jumping jacks and static stretching along with a five-minute walk-jog sequence.

General Test Administration

To ensure valid results, use the same procedure for each test for each youth every time you perform assessments. Two basic tasks are necessary for general test administration.

- **Task 1. Using correct procedure.** Always use the correct procedure. Shortcuts and incorrect procedures invalidate a test. Administer each test as it was originally designed to be applied.
- **Task 2. Monitoring and motivating youths during testing.** Monitor youth for any physical problems, such as chest pain, and for correct exercise form. Encourage youths to make their best efforts.

The specific testing procedures for each of the physical fitness tests are in appendix A. Remember to give tests in the recommended order so that the amount of exertion to perform one test doesn't influence the taking of another test.

Conclusion

The screening and fitness assessment elements should be the first two program steps. Without an accurate picture of the participants' current physical functioning you can't design a program that is both safe and effective.

Unfortunately, in some programs, especially in school settings, the physical fitness curriculum is nothing but fitness testing. Youth do not respond to that limited a focus and, in turn, do not increase their levels of fitness. So present the assessment process as just the initial component of a total program. It's the total program—both activity sessions and educational classes—that will encourage youth to exercise and increase fitness.

Chapter 5

Exercise Programming

A total physical fitness program has many elements, including group and individual exercise and educational and discussion activities, all of which can be utilized to accomplish many objectives beyond merely increasing fitness. The primary activity in implementing physical training programs, however, is structured exercise. Individual exercise programming will be discussed in chapter 6 as an educational activity. Thus, the focus of this chapter is on group exercise activities. The goal is to provide youth with the strenuous physical activity that will not only increase their levels of fitness but also introduce the habit of leading a healthy lifestyle. The objectives of the group exercise class are as follows:

- To provide a structured exercise class that increases strength, flexibility, and cardiovascular endurance
- To provide a constructive support group to encourage and reinforce physical activities
- To provide opportunities to practice self-discipline, respect, personal responsibility, and leading and following skills
- To provide a pleasurable exercise experience so that youths will sustain a physical training program over time

As we have discussed, my experience has shown that leadership is a key factor in the success of an exercise program. As a consequence, the exercise program should be directed by a strong leader or instructor. Indeed, the program should be the leaders' responsibility. Remember, group exercise classes with strong leadership are the preferred mode for getting youth involved in exercise that will increase physical fitness and, in turn, positively affect other factors, such as self-esteem and values.

Still, the development of self-esteem, self-discipline, and personal responsibility must ultimately be an individual matter. Ideally, we would expect youths to provide their own direction and motivation for maintaining exercise. The level of functioning of most at-risk youth, however, is such that you must initially direct them to undertake proper exercise, providing the discipline and responsibility they lack. In other words, the first step usually must be an "other-directed" as opposed to "inner-directed" step. Once youth successfully proceed through exercise classes, allow them to earn the right to make decisions about the class activities and to direct themselves during activity.

In order to accomplish the exercise class objectives, it is necessary to be familiar with the following:

- The principles of exercise
- Exercise class guidelines
- Exercise class routine guidelines
- Exercise safety guidelines

The aim of this chapter is to provide the guidelines for these four areas to help you design your own exercise programming systematically.

Principles of Exercise

We can view exercise as a stimulus for producing a series of physiological effects. The challenge is to design exercise activities so that the training effect increases physical fitness. All activities should follow four general principles of training:

1. **Specificity.** Physical training is very specific to the fitness area trained and to the specific movements that occur. For example, weight training will increase strength but not increase cardiovascular endurance.
2. **Overload.** Physical training must progressively place a greater demand on the body for fitness increases to occur.
3. **Regularity.** For physical training to have an effect, it must be performed on a regular basis.
4. **Individual progression.** For an individual to safely exercise, the activity must both be at the correct workload for his or her current fitness level as well as allow for a gradual increase in workload over time.

Specific and progressive training is required to increase each fitness area. Threshold values represent the minimum workload required to produce a training effect for each fitness area. Workload is defined in terms of frequency of activity, intensity of the activity, time or duration of activity, and type or mode of activity.

Frequency	=	How often
Intensity	=	How hard
Time	=	How long (duration)
Type	=	What kind of activity or mode

Table 5.1

Guidelines for Exercise Threshold Values

CARDIOVASCULAR ENDURANCE

Frequency	Intensity	Time	Type
At least 3 days per week	50%-80% of maximum oxygen uptake or 60%-85% of the maximum heart rate range. The maximum O_2 uptake is the total O_2 the body can use, while the heart rate range is the training range in which to do aerobic exercise.	At least 20 min. nonstop activity	Activities that involve large muscle (total body) movement in which the intensity can be controlled

WEIGHT CONTROL

Frequency	Intensity	Time	Type
At least 3 days per week	Expend at least 300 calories per workout session.	At least 20 min. nonstop activity	Activities that involve large muscle (total body) movement in which the intensity can be controlled

STRENGTH

Frequency	Intensity	Time	Type*
Every other day (at least 3 days per week)	Absolute strength—high resistance (pounds) and low repetitions (the number of times the exercise is performed). Muscular endurance— low resistance and high repetitions.	1 set, working up to and maintaining 3 sets. A set is the number of times you go through the series of exercises.	Isotonic exercises (weights, calisthenics, using the body weight and gravity as resistance), isometrics, and isokinetic exercises.

(continued)

Table 5.1

Guidelines for Exercise Threshold Values *(continued)*

FLEXIBILITY

Frequency	Intensity	Time	Type
At least 3 days per week, but can be daily	Static to the point of extensibility for which you feel the stretch but without any pain	Static stretch of 20-30 seconds for a minimum of 3 repetitions	Static passive stretch

*—**Isotonic** contractions occur when the muscle goes through the two phases of contraction (concentric when the muscle shortens and eccentric when the muscle lengthens back to normal). An example is a pull-up. When you pull up the body, the biceps contract (concentric) then lengthen (eccentric) when the body is let back down.

—**Isometric** contractions occur when the muscle shortens into a static contraction without movement. An example would be putting your hands flat on a desk and pushing down. The desk is not going to move nor will your arms. Your arms, however, will feel the fatigue of the static (nonmovement) effort.

—**Isokinetic** contractions occur when the speed of contraction is controlled and it is only concentric in nature. Special equipment is required to produce this contraction, which is normally used in orthopedic rehabilitation.

Guidelines have been developed that define the threshold values for each fitness area. Table 5.1 summarizes these guidelines.

These guidelines can serve as a check to be sure that the exercise program you provide meets the threshold values for producing the training effect. If the exercise performed meets these guidelines, then physical fitness will increase.

Exercise Class Guidelines

This section explains how to construct an effective exercise class by considering the following four factors:

- General guidelines
- Guidelines for selecting activities
- Guidelines for structuring activities
- Guidelines for sequencing activities

General Guidelines

Regardless of class structure, you should ensure that each exercise class includes the following elements:

- Warm-up and cooldown activities 5 to 10 minutes at the beginning and end of class
- Exercise in all three fitness areas, including strength, flexibility, and cardiovascular endurance, using structured exercise, group games, activities, or sports for 30 to 60 minutes
- A set sequence of different physical activities so that nonstop movement dominates the entire class period
- Leader-dependent activities with the leader both leading and monitoring the exercise class
- Verbal encouragement from the exercise leader to reinforce activity
- Structure that sometimes gives youth opportunities to lead, so they may serve as examples for others

Guidelines for Selecting Activities

We can categorize the various types of exercise class movements into the following types of activities.

- **Start-up activities:** These are activity modes to get youth on a regimented, controlled schedule, including warm-up exercises, such as deep breathing, rhythmic walking, jogging, and ballistic exercises, such as jumping jacks.
- **Conditioning exercises:** These include calisthenics, weight training exercises, or partner-assisted exercises.
- **Movement drills:** These include motor skill movements and challenge activities, such as short sprints, walking on a balance beam, ballistic jumping activities, and agility movements around obstacles.
- **Competitive relays.**
- **Rhythmical activities to music.** These include aerobic dance programs and group walking and running activities.
- **Games and contests:** These includes using obstacle courses, skill events (e.g., free throw shooting), and group games.
- **Sports:** These include team sport activities (e.g., basketball and flag football).

Next, the activities can be categorized by the extent to which they are structured.

- **Structured and highly controlled activity.** The class is structured and ordered in a systematic fashion following a set sequence. The three types of basic systematic fitness activity classes are the following:

— Exercise classes led in formation

— Exercise circuit training (calisthenics; see chapter 6)

— Continuous rhythmical exercise activity

• **Less structured activity.** More dependent on participant skill level, the three basic types of these classes are as follows:

— Aerobic rhythmic or dance classes

— Motor skill and relay activities, both individual and team

— Game activities, both individual and team

It is not possible in a book this size to present all the variety of group exercise class activities. Instead, you could examine the following resources, which outline a large number of focused fitness class activities:

Fitness Exercise for Children (1988) by Jim Stillwell and Jerry Stockard, Great Activities Publishing Co., Durham, NC

Fitness and Fun (1986) by John Bennett and Artie Kamiya, Great Activities Publishing Co., Durham, NC

The first category of activities, structured group activity classes, should be the core activity. Incorporate the less structured activities to vary your basic program, but don't make them the core fitness activity. The rationale is as follows:

• Many at-risk youth have very little structure in their lives. It is important to provide some systematic structure with continuity between daily sessions.

• The structured activity classes allow for more controlled and systematic progression to increase fitness over the course of a program.

• The less structured activities are more fun-oriented, providing welcome variety for participants.

Differing opinions exist as to the degree that a structured approach is necessary. However, when we analyze the results of programs for at-risk youth—whether the programs are fitness, educational, or counseling in nature—programs that have a great deal of structure are the ones that get positive results. How do you determine the degree of structure necessary? The level of responsibility exhibited by the youth should dictate the answer. In most settings, youth must first experience a structured process before they can responsibly participate in less structured activities.

Guidelines for Structuring Activities

You may choose from many different methods for structuring a group exercise class. The choice of method is usually dictated by five factors:

- The number of participants
- The number of staff
- The level of control required by the particular group
- The type of activities to be performed in class
- The facilities and equipment available

No right or wrong class structure exists; the choice of a structure is a judgment call. The group exercise activities that will be outlined represent sample activities that will provide you with an initial structured framework—especially helpful if you do not have much experience in leading group exercise classes. The class structures outlined here are not exhaustive but do represent approaches that have been field-tested. To begin, let's examine the variety of class formations you can apply.

For the whole class, the following formations usually work well.

- **Military formation in rows and columns.** Shown in figure 5.1, this formation is excellent for teaching exercises and warm-up and cooldown activities. You can also use this formation for stretching and calisthenic strength exercises, but it is not as good for indoor running.

  For extremely large groups, it is best to break the group into smaller squads or teams. This will help with control.

Leader

X	X	X	X	X	X	X	X
X	X	X	X	X	X	X	X
X	X	X	X	X	X	X	X
X	X	X	X	X	X	X	X
X	X	X	X	X	X	X	X
X	X	X	X	X	X	X	X

Figure 5.1 Military formation.

- **Circle formation.** The circle formation shown in figure 5.2 is good for smaller groups for all forms of activity (warm-up, cooldown, stretching, calisthenic strength exercises, and running). This formation aids smooth transitions from one activity to another, allowing for continuous rhythmical movement.

Figure 5.2 Circle formation.

- **Circuit formation.** In the circuit formation shown in figure 5.3, participants move through a series of stations, performing a specific exercise at each station. It is an excellent formation for doing a variety of exercises. The leader should monitor activity at each station by circulating among the stations while still keeping an eye on all the stations.

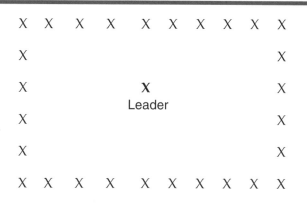

Figure 5.3 Circuit formation; leader circulates among stations, keeping an eye on all stations.

For an extremely large class the whole class should be broken down into smaller groups for some activities, such as running, circuit activities, and relays. The activity itself should determine the structure of the formation. Each smaller group performs one group activity, then moves on to the next one. For smaller groups, you can use a semicircle or circle.

Guidelines for Sequencing Activities

Sequencing is linking the flow of movement from one exercise to another (such as warm-up to aerobic exercise) with a smooth transition. Some general sequencing guidelines for an exercise class are as follows:

Warm-up	Gradually increase intensity. Use a variety of exercises. Include all body parts.
Flexibility	Do flexibility stretching exercises. Make the final activity walking, then go immediately into the cardiovascular endurance phase.
Cardiovascular endurance	Increase intensity gradually. Attempt to make the main activity continuous. Maintain movement into the strength phase.
Strength	Work all body parts by following a routine of exercises.
Other activity	Maintain continuous movement.
Cooldown	Gradually decrease activity intensity. Finish up with some stretching.

Regardless of what the major conditioning activity is (cardiovascular endurance, strength, games, or sports), make sure to include transitions between the warm-up and the major conditioning activity and between the major conditioning activity and the cooldown.

Exercise Routines

A way of viewing an exercise routine is that it is an outline or "lesson plan" for leading exercise. Many kinds of group exercise routines are possible. First we'll discuss the general guidelines, then we'll examine three sample routines.

General Guidelines

Outline the routine in writing, providing enough specific direction to clearly define the structure of the activity. You should include a "general concept" section explaining the routine and an "activity process" section describing the sequence of activities and exercises and their time frames.

Sample Class Routines

The following outlines describe three different exercise routines that have been used successfully with at-risk youth: continuous rhythmical exercise, military formation, and circuit training. These represent the most structured of the various group exercise routines discussed. In addition, these routines have tended to be the most popular for both youth and leaders.

Exercise Class 1

Continuous Rhythmical Exercise

GENERAL CONCEPT

This routine is ideal for

- a gym floor or outside setting,
- nonstop activity the entire period,
- covering all fitness areas, and
- allowing youth of differing fitness levels to participate in the same activities but at their own pace.

ACTIVITY PROCESS

Guidelines

- Assign participants to a gear level based on their fitness assessment results on the one-mile run. Those in low gear are below the 50th percentile; those in high gear are at 50th percentile or above.
- You lead the activity at first, later selecting participants to take over segments to lead.

- The standard exercise period runs as follows:
  — Warm-up
  — Flexibility conditioning circle
  — Cardiovascular endurance walk-run
  — Muscular endurance (calisthenics) conditioning circle
  — Cardiovascular endurance walk-run
  — Cooldown

Routine Elements

The elements of this routine are as follows:

Warm-up. You can use a large circle, leading the warm-up exercises yourself. You can also select participants to take turns leading warm-up exercises.

Flexibility and muscular endurance (calisthenics) conditioning circle. For the flexibility and the muscular endurance routines, bring the group into a conditioning circle while you stand in the middle (see figure 5.2). You can use a single circle or concentric circles, depending on the number of participants. As group members finish an exercise, have them get up and walk around the circle until everybody finishes and is ready it start a new exercise. This maintains continuous movement.
   You can select participants to go into the middle of the circle and lead the class.

Cardiovascular endurance walk-run. For the cardiovascular endurance routine, the walk-run course can be an oval (either a gym or a marked course outside). You should lead the faster participants (high gear) on the walk-run sequence, following the outer edge of the oval. Have slower participants (low gear) do their laps on the inner part of the oval. You can select participants at different times to lead the group.

Cooldown. You can use a large circle. Stand in the middle to lead the cooldown exercises. Once again, you can select participants to take turns leading.

Routine Sequence

Time/Activity	Low gear	High gear
5-minute warm-up	Walking	Walking
	Arm swings	Arm swings
	Deep breathing	Deep breathing
	Jumping jacks	Jumping jacks
5-minute flexibility	Hamstrings stretch	Hamstrings stretch
	Knee pull	Knee pull
	Trunk bender	Trunk bender
	Calf stretch	Calf stretch
	Thigh stretch	Thigh stretch

(continued)

Continuous Rhythmical Exercise *(continued)*

10-minute endurance walk-run	Walk 3, jog 1 (Laps)	Walk 1, jog 3 (Laps)
15-minute muscular endurance	5 reps Sit-ups Push-ups Calf raises Three-quarter knee bends Back extensions Dips Leg curls	15 reps Sit-ups Push-ups Calf raises Three-quarter knee bends Back extensions Dips Leg curls
10-minute endurance walk-run	Walk 3, jog 1 (Laps)	Walk 1, jog 3 (Laps)
5-minute cooldown	Walking Arm swings Deep breathing	Walking Arm swings Deep breathing

Progression

As participants improve fitness levels, increase the workload gradually. For example, increase sets and repetitions for strength conditioning. And during the walk-run sequence, the entire time period could be jogging.

Military Formation Exercise

GENERAL CONCEPT

This routine is ideal for

- teaching correct exercise form,
- allowing the leader to control the entire group, and
- working with a large number of participants.

ACTIVITY PROCESS

Guidelines

- Stand in front of the group and lead every exercise (see figure 5.1). Have participants perform all exercises while in position within the formation.
- The standard exercise period runs as follows:
  — Warm-up
  — Flexibility (static stretching)
  — Calisthenics
  — Cooldown

Routine Sequence

Time	Activity
5-10 minutes	Warm-up activities
5-10 minutes	Flexibility (static stretching)
10-15 minutes	Calisthenic exercises
5-10 minutes	Cooldown activities

Optional running in place sequence

Time	Activity
5-10 minutes	Warm-up activities
10-15 minutes	Flexibility (static stretching) Run in place for 30 seconds between each exercise
15-20 minutes	Calisthenic exercises Run in place for 30 seconds between each exercise
5-10 minutes	Cooldown activities and stretches

Progression

As participants improve fitness levels, increase the workload gradually. For example, increase sets and repetitions for flexibility and strength conditioning. You can select members of the group to come to the front of the class and lead exercises.

Super Circuit

GENERAL CONCEPT

This routine can be performed using calisthenics, weight training exercises, or motor skill exercises, such as jumping, skipping, or dodging around chairs. It allows each participant to move at his or her own pace.

ACTIVITY PROCESS

Guidelines

- Assign participants a standard training dose of 5 to 10 repetitions of each exercise, building the program up over time.
- You do not lead the exercise but monitor participants, moving around the exercise space.
- Set up the circuit so that each participant has his or her own station. Organize stations in a rectangle on the floor (see figure 5.3). Have each participant perform one exercise at his or her own station, then jog around the exercise area for 30 seconds, and finally return to his or her station to do the next exercise.

Routine Sequence

Time	Activity
5-10 minutes	Leader-led warm-up exercise with walk-jog.
30 minutes	Circuit for three sets: You can create a circuit that includes calisthenic exercises, weight training exercises (see chapter 6 for more on these two types of exercise), or motor skill activities, such as jumping, balancing on one foot, and performing agility circles. (Those who complete the circuit ahead of others can jog or walk around the group until everyone finishes.)
5-10 minutes	Cool down individually immediately after finishing the circuit.

Progression

Keep the routine the same over time, but have the participants add one to two repetitions to each exercise each week.

These three group exercise class routines are examples. The key issue is to establish an exercise class process and class structure, then incorporate a variety of activities over time to maintain interest and enthusiasm.

Exercise Safety Guidelines

A major function of fitness program management is to ensure the safety of participants. The goal of safety programming is for all program procedures to follow prudent safety guidelines. Written safety guidelines should be in place to give staff necessary direction for all aspects of the physical training program. The following are six areas for which you should define specific safety procedures:

- Staff assignment and training guidelines
- Screening guidelines
- Warm-up and cooldown guidelines
- Injury prevention guidelines
- Environmental guidelines
- Emergency procedures

Staff Assignment and Training Guidelines

Only those staff who have been trained to provide physical training programs should be assigned to deliver the program. These training and assignment guidelines should be in writing. (See chapter 9 for more specific guidelines.)

Screening Guidelines

Screening is the data gathering process to determine if it is safe for an individual to participate in physical activity. Having written screening guidelines that define who can and cannot participate is necessary (see also chapter 4). Special attention should be given to youth who have the following health problems:

- Cardiovascular disease
- Diabetes
- Respiratory disorders
- Epilepsy
- Orthopedic conditions
- Medication use

If these conditions are present, make sure you follow a review process that requires a physician's approval before participation.

Warm-Up and Cooldown Guidelines

Warm-up is the segment of an exercise session in which a transition from inactivity to intense activity takes place. The warm-up should be a gradual process, allowing the body to make the physiological (breathing, muscle movement, hormonal) changes and hemodynamic (blood flow) changes necessary to perform intense activity. A proper warm-up helps prevent injury.

The two basic types of warm-up exercises involve general and specific exercises. General warm-up exercises are general movements that increase blood flow regardless of the type of activity the warm-up precedes, e.g., walking, jogging, deep breathing, arm swings, and total body ballistic (dynamic) movements. Specific warm-up exercises are exercises that directly relate to the activity the warm-up precedes, e.g., static stretching for those areas that will be involved in the main activity, such as Achilles tendon stretching before running, and rehearsal of the activity itself, such as jumping and shooting before playing basketball.

Cooldown is the segment of the exercise session during which the metabolism of the body gradually returns back to the normal resting state. The cooldown period allows the body to gradually redistribute the blood flow from the working muscles to the remainder of the body. During a proper cooldown, a gradual decrease in hormone levels reduces the blood pressure and heart rate. Relaxation is enhanced to minimize the tightening of muscles after activity. By gradually cooling down rather than simply stopping all activity abruptly, the problem of blood pooling in the extremities, which may cause dizziness or fainting, is avoided. Use the same exercises for the cooldown as you used for the warm-up.

Ideally, the warm-up and cooldown phases of the exercise session should last between 5 to 10 minutes at the beginning and end of the workout session.

Injury Prevention Guidelines

The guidelines to prevent injury cover the following five areas:

• **Hazard control.** This relates to controlling sources of potential injuries. Guidelines should cover the supervision and maintenance of equipment and the monitoring and controlling of environmental factors, such as heat, humidity, and cold.

• **Staff knowledge of participants' risk factors.** Staff need to be knowledgeable about participants' exercise risk factors by reviewing information from health screening and fitness assessment.

• **Participant education.** Participants need to be educated about topics such as proper exercise techniques for stretching, lifting, and aerobic activities; proper use of equipment; how to modify exercise to fit the environment; how to prevent and identify injuries; and proper exercise progression. Participants should always warm up before and cool down after fitness assessments and exercise sessions.

• **Participant exercise plans.** Exercise routines should be appropriate to participants' current fitness levels and progressive.

• **Participant monitoring.** Staff need to observe and supervise all participant activity, watching for signs of stress and potential injury situations. Focus monitoring on two major areas: cardiovascular stress and overuse.

Cardiovascular Stress Danger Signals

- Pain or pressure in the chest
- Dizziness
- Irregular heartbeat
- Shortness of breath
- Pain or numbness along either arm
- Persistent fatigue
- Nausea
- Failure of pulse to recover

Overuse Signals

- Unexplained soreness
- Lowered resistance to disease
- Colds, headaches, cold sores
- Chronic fatigue
- Depression or frustration related to effort
- Lowered coordination levels

Exercise leaders must keep in position to be able to observe all participants on a regular basis. The "talk test" is a simple tool that staff can use to check if participants are overexerting themselves. If an individual cannot carry on a conversation while performing exercise, then the exercise is too strenuous.

Environmental Guidelines

Environmental conditions can have a significant impact on exercise safety and exercise performance. It normally takes 30 days for an individual to fully adjust to a new environment. The three general program guidelines for environmental safety are as follows:

- Establish written procedures for exercise in different environmental situations.
- Educate participants as to environmental considerations.
- When possible, control the exercise environment.

Programming must account for four major environmental factors: heat and humidity, cold, altitude, and pollution. Controlling for or adapting to the four environmental factors is a major concern for safety programming.

Heat and Humidity. When we exercise in excessive and prolonged heat, the body's cooling mechanisms can break down. The three heat illnesses that can develop from heat stress are heat cramps, heat exhaustion, and heatstroke:

- With heat cramps, the muscles cramp and the skin may become sweaty. It is not a serious condition, although the person should get out of the heat and drink some water.
- Heat exhaustion includes heavy sweating, nausea, and weakness. The person should get out of the heat, drink water (if conscious), and receive medical help as soon as possible.
- Heatstroke, the most serious condition, can be life-threatening because the body's temperature regulating mechanisms no longer work. Symptoms include a total lack of sweating; an elevated temperature, an elevated heart rate, which may decrease; reddened skin; and disorientation. Rush a person in this condition to the hospital immediately for cooling and professional care.

To help avoid these illnesses, follow these four major hot weather training guidelines:

- **Water.** Exercisers must continuously replenish their fluid levels to avoid heat stress problems. They should drink as much as they can tolerate before, during, and after exercise. Special sports drinks with carbohydrates and electrolytes are usually not necessary; water gets to the muscles more quickly. Salt tablets are also not necessary.
- **Clothing.** Clothing should allow maximal evaporation to occur, so exercisers should wear loose and absorbent materials. They should also choose light-colored clothing to reflect the heat. Exercisers should never wear rubber or plastic suits.

- **Training intensity.** Modify training to allow participants to acclimatize (about 30 days). Warn exercisers to not expect their regular levels of exercise performance. Reduce exercise intensity and duration.
- **Monitoring the heat.** Monitor heat stress by using heat stress indicators such as the temperature and humidity index. Add the temperature and humidity together for a reading, then compare it with the index. (Humidity is a problem because it does not allow evaporation, and thus cooling, to occur.) Usually a heat index of 130 to 140 degrees Fahrenheit is in the extreme caution zone. When the reading is in the extreme caution zone, curtail or avoid exercise.

Cold. Cold is a stressor that can also cause physical problems and even death. Cold places a burden on the body for temperature regulation and circulation and can impact either peripheral body parts or the central core. The problem that affects peripheral body parts is frostbite, in which extremities such as toes and fingers freeze. The more serious and life-threatening problem is hypothermia, in which the total body temperature falls to 95 degrees Fahrenheit or below. In either case, should you suspect such a condition, you should seek medical help immediately.

To help avoid such problems, follow these four major cold weather training guidelines:

- **Water and food.** The problem in the cold is keeping the core temperature up, so exercisers should eat plenty of carbohydrates to feed the body's cold weather metabolism, which is higher than in warmer weather. Dehydration also can be a problem in cold weather, so exercisers should drink plenty of fluids and avoid alcohol.
- **Clothing.** Clothing must afford protection while not trapping sweat. Exercisers should dress in layers so they can remove layers as body temperature rises. They should also wear an outer layer that is wind resistant, including a hat.
- **Training intensity.** Exercisers need to keep moving while outside so they stay warm. They may work at a lower intensity, but they need to keep moving!
- **Wind chill.** Wind chill makes the cold more dangerous as cold is accentuated by high wind. For example, a temperature of 32 degrees Fahrenheit with a 25 mile per hour wind feels like 0 degrees. Wind chill levels are reported on the news as the "wind chill index."

Altitude. At higher elevations, the air contains less oxygen; consequently you must work harder to maintain a given level of activity. The major effects of altitude first appear between 5000 and 7000 feet. The body adapts to altitude by developing more red blood cells so it can distribute more of the limited oxygen. Until this acclimatization occurs, however, any given workload will be more demanding.

The major problem with altitude is altitude sickness, which occurs when a person is physically active at an altitude he or she is not acclimatized to. Symptoms of altitude sickness include headache, nausea, and mental confusion. Treat the victim by providing water to drink, keeping him or her warm, and going to a lower elevation. Hypothermia can also occur at higher elevations.

To adjust to altitude, follow these four major altitude training guidelines:

- **Water.** As with other training environments this is vital.
- **Clothing.** Clothing should be the same as for cold weather.
- **Training intensity.** Generally it needs to be lowered.
- **Monitoring.** Exercisers need to keep track of the wind chill.

Pollution. The major pollution problem is similar to the problem of altitude in that not enough oxygen is in the air, this time because of competing pollutants. This makes exercise more difficult as well as potentially harmful because of the ingestion of the pollutants. To help avoid these problems, follow these three major pollution training guidelines:

- **Timing of exercise.** Exercise should not occur outside from 7 to 10 A.M. and 4 to 7 P.M., which are peak traffic periods.
- **Place of exercise.** Exercisers should attempt to work out in a location with low pollution.
- **Exposure reduction.** The effects of pollution are cumulative over time. If possible, exercisers should limit exercising outdoors if in a highly polluted environment.

Emergency Procedures

A program that has well-defined emergency procedures is the last line of defense for safety. Guidelines are necessary for four main areas: preparation for emergencies, handling of emergencies, reporting, and emergency equipment.

Prepare for emergencies by following these guidelines:

- Ensure that staff are adequately trained and certified in CPR and first aid.
- Have staff practice responding to simulated emergencies every three to six months.

- Make sure necessary emergency equipment is in place and is accessible.
- Include a well-stocked first aid kit in the emergency equipment.
- Post names, addresses, and phone numbers of emergency units.
- Define, post, and review with staff your emergency procedures.

Handle emergencies based on a standard procedure that contains the following steps:

- Determination of injury
- Rendering of appropriate aid
- Notification of appropriate medical personnel (EMT, hospital, and the like)
- Arrangement for transportation
- Notification of appropriate kin, supervisors, and so on
- Reporting

Because of liability issues, you should use a standard injury or incident reporting form with the following elements to report all injuries:

- Participant's name, address, phone number, and other related information
- Place of incident
- Date and time of incident
- Description of the nature of the incident
- Site of injury
- Any vital signs information (heart rate, blood pressure, and so on)
- Description of treatment
- Disposition of the individual
- Follow-up recommendations
- Witnesses' names, addresses, and phone numbers
- Statements of witnesses

Every fitness program should have as much safety and emergency medical equipment as possible. The most basic need is for a fully stocked first aid kit. The kit should be portable and have the following basic elements:

- First aid manual
- Disposable latex gloves

- Scissors
- Tongue depressors
- Triangular bandages
- Cotton swabs
- Bandages
- Sterile gauze pads and eye pads
- Adhesive tape
- Elastic wrap
- Blanket
- Safety pins
- Cold pack or ice otherwise available
- First aid cream
- Hydrogen peroxide
- Splints
- Household bleach and water solution
- Pocket masks for CPR
- Plastic gloves

The first aid kit should be checked on a monthly basis, and supplies should be replenished as needed.

The emergency procedures for a fitness program are similar to standard emergency procedures. Preparation, anticipation, and execution are the basic elements.

Conclusion

We can reduce all the exercise guidelines to two underlying guidelines. The first is to organize the training program to produce the training effect. The positive outcomes that are desired for at-risk youth, such as positive behavior change and increased self-esteem, will only occur if a training effect increases fitness. The second guideline is that the physical training program must be delivered in a safe manner. This pertains to ensuring that participants do not perform too much or unsafe exercise. Both guidelines must be met for the physical training program to be effective.

The exercise component is the major element of a physical training program. Other elements, however, such as education to teach youth about exercise, blend with the exercise class activities. The next chapter provides guidelines on how to effectively blend educational elements with physical training.

Chapter 6

Educational Programming

While the exercise-class component is the most important activity in a physical training program, an educational component is also necessary. The goal in providing fitness education programming is to teach youth fitness assessment, goal setting, and planning—all life skills they can apply to developing a healthy lifestyle. We can define the educational objectives of a physical training program as follows:

- To teach participants the personal physical fitness program development skills of self-assessment, goal setting, exercise planning, and self-control
- To teach each participant to apply those skills to develop an individualized exercise program

The major programming element to accomplish these objectives consists of formal instruction to learn and apply fitness-assessment, goal-setting, exercise-planning, and self-control skills to develop an individual physical training or fitness program.

The group exercise element of a physical training program is, by nature, fitness leader directed. The educational element provides a framework through which youths assume more responsibility as they apply the fitness skills they have learned to design and maintain an individualized fitness program. In this sense, the educational component empowers youth to be more inner-directed within the physical training program. This chapter will provide both the guidelines for educational programming and an overview of the content of the educational component.

Life Skills Instruction

The focus of instruction should be on helping the youth learn to design their own personal physical training or fitness program. The instructional units should be short, self-contained modules of not more than 15 minutes.

It is best to present the instructional units during class directly after the exercise component. Instruction should focus on the youth performing a "do" step as part of the unit, such as filling out a form to set goals or to outline an exercise plan. A participant workbook helps youth apply the skills they learn to designing their own programs.

The essential topic areas in which to provide instruction are as follows:

Topic	Life Skills
Health screening	Assessing yourself by evaluating health problems
Physical fitness assessment	Assessing yourself by taking fitness tests
Fitness goal setting	Comparing yourself to norms by profiling fitness test scores
	Setting fitness improvement goals
Exercise planning	Planning ahead by outlining exercise plans
Self-control	Controlling behavior by applying self-monitoring and contracting techniques

Due to space limitations, only those topics that are essential to helping youth develop the life skills necessary to planning their own physical training programs are presented. However, you can cover many topics in a total fitness program, such as nutrition and weight control. Specific guidelines for how to transfer the fitness life skill material to other topics, such as substance abuse, are also presented.

All youth need to develop the ability to stop and think before acting. Too often, unfortunately, the at-risk youth does the opposite: act, or more accurately, react first, think later. One way to confront this destructive process is to organize the various life skill instructional units to teach a basic four-step process for controlling one's own behavior in the context of developing a personal physical training or fitness program, as shown in figure 6.1.

In the rest of this chapter, each life skill area is presented in detail, covering the following three elements:

- Youth learning "do" steps. This will outline what the participants should be doing in the educational module.
- Guidelines or procedures for implementing the module.
- Sample forms that help to organize the "do" steps.

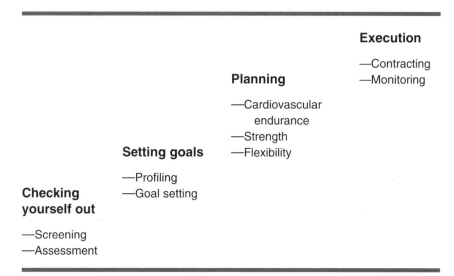

Figure 6.1 The four-step process for creating a personal physical training program.

Screening

The screening process was already discussed in detail in chapter 4, but here we look at it from the educational perspective. Screening can teach youth to recognize important health areas and how their own health status can affect how they function physically and otherwise. This process sets the stage for youth to look critically and introspectively at themselves.

"Do" Steps for Screening

The "do" step for youth in this process is to fill out informed consent and health screening forms (see chapter 4). This forces them to look at themselves, encouraging introspection. They become actively involved in the process of "checking themselves out."

Screening Education Guidelines

Whenever possible, each youth should fill out the forms by him or herself. If that is not possible because of reading or writing difficulties, then have someone read the questions to the youth for him or her to answer orally. Use the questions and discussions about the health areas on the health history form to make the youth more aware of how health status affects how he or she functions and how exercise can affect those health areas.

Screening is a necessary process for any youth who engages in an exercise program. The educational process uses the screening process to teach youth to assess their own health.

Physical Fitness Assessment

The physical fitness assessment process discussed in chapter 4 is an important educational module as well. Teaching youth how to take and administer the fitness tests to themselves also helps them become more introspective.

"Do" Steps for Physical Fitness Assessment

Youths perform two "do" steps during assessment. The first is to take the fitness tests, learning how to take the tests so they can assess themselves in the future. The second "do" step is to have them record their raw scores (the scores they achieved on the tests) on a fitness profile form. Both of these "do" steps force youth to participate actively in the assessment process rather than as passive recipients of a service.

Fitness Education Guidelines

Use a formal fitness assessment form to document performance in the fitness tests. Figure 6.2 shows an example of a form filled in for a 13-year-old boy. This same form is used to teach youth the next goal-setting step, which is to profile their scores.

If the goal is to teach youths to administer the assessments themselves, time must be dedicated to teach them how to do each fitness assessment. One way to accomplish this is to allow them to practice testing each other. In this way, youth begin to own the assessment process for themselves—a benefit that doesn't occur when someone in authority records the scores for them.

Profiling and Goal Setting

Once the assessment is done, teach youth to profile the results and set goals. A fitness goal defines the expectations for maintaining and improving fitness. Characteristics of this process are as follows:

- Goal setting should be individualized in that each goal is defined in relation to the level at which the individual is currently functioning, based on fitness assessment tests.
- Goal setting should be systematic and progressive so that the youth can set reasonable, achievable expectations.

Fitness Profile

Fitness Test Results

Test	Score	Category
% body fat	*12.5*	_____
Push-ups	*18*	_____
Sit-and-reach	*10.5*	_____
Sit-ups	*41*	_____
One-mile run	*8:00*	_____

Test	Above average	Average	Below average
% body fat	_____	_____	_____
Push-ups	_____	_____	_____
Sit-and-reach	_____	_____	_____
Sit-ups	_____	_____	_____
One-mile run	_____	_____	_____

Figure 6.2 Sample physical fitness profile form showing fitness test results.

- Goal setting should be motivating, defining progressive milestones for improvement.
- Goal setting should be an introspective process in that it forces the individual to look at himself or herself objectively.
- Goal setting should make the individual accountable to himself or herself for changing his or her own behavior.

"Do" Steps for Goal Setting

Youth perform two basic "do" steps at this stage. The first is to profile their fitness test scores. This involves showing them how to compare their raw scores to a norm profile. This helps them to objectively compare themselves to others. The second step is to help them define their fitness test improvement goals. Both of these steps require youth to use fitness assessment forms, such as the sample fitness profile and goal-setting forms (see figures 6.3, page 99, and 6.4, page 100). The goal-setting process helps youth learn to put plans into operation that will help them improve in a reasonably progressive manner.

Fitness Profiling Guidelines

A test score, the raw score, does not have any meaning by itself. It must be compared to a norm or standard. A norm indicates how an individual's performance relates to the scores of a similar age and gender group, the norm group. The process of using a norm chart to see whether a score is above, at, or below the average score for the norm group is known as "profiling."

To make this an educational process, have the youth use the norm charts to categorize their performances by following these steps:

1. Find the norm chart for sex and age for each test (table 6.1).
2. Fill in the blank for the fitness category (above average, average, below average) that is closest to the raw score on the top of the fitness profile form (figure 6.3).
3. Plot the scores on the fitness profile form by placing an "X" under each test in the block for its category.

Table 6.1 presents the norm charts. The norms for the one-mile run, sit-ups, sit-and-reach, and skinfold measurement tests are from the American Alliance for Health, Physical Education, Recreation and Dance (1). The push-up norms come from the First Choice fitness program (2). Figure 6.3 shows the profile form filled out for the same 13-year-old boy mentioned earlier.

Goal-Setting Guidelines

The second element of goal setting is the setting of fitness improvement goals. To make this an educational process, have youth set goals, using a goal-setting form. Design the process to encourage youth to expect realistic improvements and to recognize that time is necessary to reach a goal. The steps to goal setting are as follows:

1. Use a goal-setting form such as that shown in figure 6.4 (page 100). Fill in the current fitness category for each test, using the information recorded on the fitness profile form (figure 6.3).
2. Fill in the fitness goal category using the following guidelines:
   - If the score is below average, make the goal average.
   - If the score is above average, then maintaining that is the goal.
   - If the score is average, make the goal above average.

Table 6.1

Fitness Test Norms

PERCENT BODY FAT

					Age				
	%	10	11	12	13	14	15	16	17
Category									
				Male					
Above	51%+	12.1–	14.1–	13.1–	13.1–	12.1–	12.1–	12.1–	13.1–
Average	50%	12.2	14.2	13.2	13.2	12.2	12.2	12.2	13.2
Below	49%–	12.3+	14.3+	13.3+	13.3+	12.3+	12.3+	12.3+	13.3+
				Female					
Above	51%+	18.1–	19.1–	19.1–	19.7–	23.4–	24.4–	24.2–	24.2–
Average	50%	18.2	19.2	19.2	19.8	23.5	24.5	24.3	24.3
Below	49%–	18.3+	19.3+	19.3+	19.9+	23.6+	24.6+	24.4+	24.4+

PUSH-UPS

					Age				
	%	10	11	12	13	14	15	16	17
Category									
				Male					
Above	51%+	22+	24+	25+	26+	27+	28+	29+	34+
Average	50%	21	23	24	25	26	27	28	33
Below	49%–	20–	22–	23–	24–	25–	26–	27–	32–
				Female					
Above	51%+	18+	19+	20+	21+	22+	23+	23+	27+
Average	50%	17	18	19	20	21	22	22	26
Below	49%–	16–	17–	18–	19–	20–	21–	21–	25–

SIT-AND-REACH (in.)

					Age				
	%	10	11	12	13	14	15	16	17
Category									
				Male					
Above	51%+	9.9+	9.9+	10.3+	10.3+	11.1+	11.9+	11.9+	13.5+

(continued)

Table 6.1

Fitness Test Norms *(continued)*

	%								
Average	50%	9.8	9.8	10.2	10.2	11.0	11.8	11.8	13.4
Below	49%–	9.7–	9.7–	10.1–	10.1–	10.9–	11.7–	11.7–	13.3–

Female

	%								
Above	51%+	11.1+	11.5+	11.9+	12.3+	13.0+	14.3+	13.5+	13.9+
Average	50%	11.0	11.4	11.8	12.2	12.9	14.2	13.4	13.8
Below	49%–	10.9–	11.3–	11.7–	12.1–	12.8–	14.1–	13.3–	13.7–

SIT-UPS

Age

Category	%	10	11	12	13	14	15	16	17

Male

	%	10	11	12	13	14	15	16	17
Above	51%+	35+	38+	40+	42+	43+	45+	46+	47+
Average	50%	34	37	39	41	42	44	45	46
Below	49%–	33–	36–	38–	40–	41–	43–	44–	45–

Female

	%	10	11	12	13	14	15	16	17
Above	51%+	33+	35+	37+	36+	36+	38+	34+	38+
Average	50%	32	34	36	35	35	37	33	37
Below	49%–	31–	34–	35–	34–	34–	36–	32–	36–

ONE-MILE RUN

Age

Category	%	10	11	12	13	14	15	16	17

Male

	%	10	11	12	13	14	15	16	17
Above	51%+	9:18–	9:05–	8:19–	7:26–	7:09–	7:13–	7:10–	7:24–
Average	50%	9:19	9:06	8:20	7:27	7:10	7:14	7:11	7:25
Below	49%–	9:20+	9:07+	8:21+	7:28+	7:11+	7:15+	7:12+	7:26+

Female

	%	10	11	12	13	14	15	16	17
Above	51%+	11:05–	10:26–	9:46–	9:26–	9:34–	10:04–	10:44–	9:46–
Average	50%	11:06	10:27	9:47	9:27	9:35	10:05	10:45	9:47
Below	49%–	11:07+	10:28+	9:48+	9:28+	9:36+	10:06+	10:46+	9:48+

All norms except push-ups reprinted with permission from the *Physical Best Education Kit*, 1996. The *Physical Best Education Kit* is a publication of the American Alliance for Health, Physical Education, Recreation and Dance, 1900 Association Drive, Reston, VA 20191.

Fitness Profile

Fitness Test Results

Test	Score	Category
% body fat	*12.5*	*Above Average*
Push-ups	*18*	*Below Average*
Sit-and-reach	*10.5*	*Above Average*
Sit-ups	*41*	*Average*
One-mile run	*8:00*	*Below Average*

Test	Above average	Average	Below average
% body fat	X	____	____
Push-ups	____	____	X
Sit-and-reach	X	____	____
Sit-ups	____	X	____
One-mile run	____	____	X

Figure 6.3 Sample physical fitness profile form showing profiling information.

3. Fill in the goal score for each test. This sets the score you want to achieve the next time you take the fitness test. You will need to review the norm charts for each test. Locate the raw or test score you must achieve to be at that level and record it on the goal-setting form.

- If the goal is to become average, then the goal score is that score required to be average on the chart. *Note:* If the current test score is less than half the goal score to become average, then the goal score needs to be broken down into smaller increments. For example, if the 13-year-old boy scored 10 on the sit-up test, he could break down the goal score to first obtain a score of 25 before trying to reach the average goal of 41.

- If the goal is to be above average, set the goal score along the following guidelines:

Sit-ups and push-ups = 5-10 repetitions above current score

Sit-and-reach = 1-2 inches above current score

$$\% \text{ body fat } = \text{ 1-2 \% below current score}$$

$$\text{One-mile run } = \text{ 30 seconds to 1 minute below current score}$$

4. Fill in the date of the next fitness assessment where you will check yourself out to see if you have reached your goals. Normally, an 8- to 10-week time period is enough time to see improvement toward a goal. Figure 6.4 shows an example for the same 13-year-old boy.

The goal-setting process is a chance for youth to experience sitting down and thinking through goals. It forces them to look at reasonable expectations and to look at the future in terms of a time frame. This process can have the effect of getting youth to think before they act, to plan for results, and to expect results.

Exercise Planning

A simplified way of viewing the screening and assessment educational elements of designing an individual program is that they help the individual to define where he or she is. The goal-setting element helps to define where he or she needs to be. The exercise planning process helps to define how to get there.

Fitness Goal Setting

Fitness Category

	Current category	Goal category	Goal score
% body fat	Above Average	Above Average	12.5
Push-ups	Below Average	Average	24
Sit-and-reach	Above Average	Above Average	10.5
Sit-ups	Average	Above Average	51
One-mile run	Below Average	Average	7:27

Date of next fitness testing: In 8 weeks

Figure 6.4 Sample completed fitness goal-setting form.

"Do" Steps for Exercise Planning

The specific "do" steps involve having youth outline exercise routines for each of three fitness areas: cardiovascular endurance, strength, and flexibility. (See chapter 1 for definitions of each area.) Teach youth that each fitness area has its own type of exercise training and how to design their own appropriate routines.

Cardiovascular Endurance Training Guidelines

To develop cardiovascular endurance, you must increase your capacity to utilize oxygen. Thus, the cardiovascular endurance training must force the body to perform work so that large amounts of oxygen are used. The body will change to adapt to the training in a variety of structural and functional ways so that the cardiovascular system can supply more oxygen to the working muscles and so that the muscles are able to utilize more oxygen.

Aerobic training activities are those activities that have a high energy cost, referring to the amount of energy (and oxygen) the body utilizes performing the activity. Cardiovascular training activities

- require large amounts of oxygen,
- use the whole body,
- use large muscle groups,
- are rhythmical for sustained activity, and
- can be monitored and controlled in terms of duration and intensity.

Activities can be classified as major or secondary aerobic activities, with the major activities using more energy than the secondary activities. Major and secondary cardiovascular endurance activities include the following:

Major Activities	Secondary Activities
Running	Group exercise classes
Brisk walking	Basketball
Cycling	Racquet sports
Swimming	
Cross country skiing	

Two methods for defining a cardiovascular endurance training routine for youth are heart rate training and aerobic points training.

Heart Rate Training. This is a method whereby you can use the training heart rate to define and monitor intensity of work, regardless of type of activity. The heart rate is a good indicator of oxygen consumption in that the higher the heart rate, the more oxygen consumed. Consequently, it is possible to use exercise heart rate to monitor work effort. It is the least sophisticated but most appropriate for the sedentary first time exerciser. Four steps outline this routine.

1. Select an exercise mode or activity (running, cycling, or the like).
2. Determine training heart rate as follows:
   - Calculate estimated maximal heart rate as 220 minus the participant's age.
   - Multiply the estimated maximal heart rate by .7 (70%) to determine the target heart rate.
   - Determine a 10-second pulse rate for the training heart rate by dividing the target heart rate by 6.
3. Perform the aerobic exercise for at least 20 minutes nonstop at the training heart rate.
4. Perform the routine at least three times a week.

Two additional steps help apply this routine:

1. It is best to give the individual a heart rate training zone to stay at instead of one number. To do this add and subtract one beat to the 10-second pulse training heart rate.
2. The individual must determine the exercise pace for maintaining that heart rate training zone.
   - Take the pulse rate 5 to 10 minutes after beginning the aerobic routine (this ensures the participant has been exercising at a steady rate).
   - Take the pulse rate immediately for only 10 seconds (after any greater length of time, the heart rate is recovering and an accurate exercise rate will not be obtained).
   - If the pulse rate is too high, slow the pace down; if it is too low, speed up the pace.

Figure 6.5 shows a sample training heart rate calculation for the 13-year-old boy.

Aerobic Points Training. This is a method whereby points are assigned to a variety of activities for their intensity and duration. This approach emphasizes meeting specific performance goals. The aerobic points system, developed by Dr. Ken Cooper, allows a comparison across a

Determining Training Heart Rate

(Running mode)

Age	13
Maximal heart rate	220
	−13
	207
70% intensity	207
	x .7
	144.9
10-second pulse rate	145 ÷ 6 = 24.1
	(Round off to 24)

Figure 6.5 Sample training heart rate calculation.

variety of activities. If two different activities (e.g., running one mile in 8 minutes and swimming 600 yards in 15 minutes) have the same aerobic points (five), then they can be compared for equivalent aerobic effort.

The aerobic points system is based on an individual earning at least 30 to 35 points per week, determined by preliminary research on this system, which indicated that people who earned at least 30 to 35 points per week tended to be in the good or better aerobic fitness categories. Two books by Dr. Ken Cooper contain aerobic points exercise schedules for over 30 different activities:

The Aerobics Program for Total Well Being (1983), published by M. Evans (New York)

Kid Fitness (1991), Bantam Books (New York)

To use the aerobic points system, the participant simply selects an activity, then follows the daily and weekly schedule. As with heart rate training, a participant must perform the exercise at least three days a week for a minimum of 20 minutes. Table 6.2 presents an example of a running program that gradually increases the aerobic points for the 13-year-old boy.

Table 6.2

Sample Aerobic Points Running Program

Week	Activity	Distance	Time	Frequency/week	Points/week
1	Walking	1.5 miles	30:00	3	6
2	Walking	2.0 miles	40:00	3	9
3	Walk-jog	2.0 miles	35:00	3	9
4	Walk-jog	2.0 miles	30:00	3	15
5	Jogging	2.0 miles	25:00	3	15
6	Jogging	2.0 miles	22:00	3	21
7	Jogging	2.5 miles	30:00	3	27
8	Jogging	2.5 miles	27:00	3	27
9	Jogging	3.0 miles	32.00	3	33
10	Jogging	3.0 miles	31:00	3	33

Data from *The aerobics program for total well being*, Ken Cooper, 1983, pp. 247-258 (New York: M. Evans Company).

Strength Training Guidelines

Two general types of strength exist, and both are required for day-to-day living and for physical performance:

- Absolute strength—a muscle's ability to generate maximum force in one contraction
- Muscular endurance (or dynamic strength)—a muscle's ability to make repeated contractions

Ideally, any strength training program should increase both types of strength. You can use two basic strength training modes: non–equipment-dependent and equipment-dependent.

Muscular endurance can be developed with non–equipment-dependent modes, but they are not as effective for developing absolute strength. The two basic non–equipment-dependent modes are isotonic and isometric training. Isotonic modes allow for both positive (concentric) contractions, in which the muscle shortens to move, and negative (eccentric) contractions, in which the muscle lengthens back to the resting position. Examples of isotonic modes are calisthenic exercises, which use body weight an gravity for resistance, and partner-assisted calisthenics. Isometric exercises involve the muscle making a static contraction against an immovable resistance, but you cannot vary the resistance.

You can easily develop both absolute strength and muscular endurance with equipment training programs. The two equipment modes are isotonic and isokinetic. Isotonic strength training equipment allows you to work against both positive and negative resistance. Examples of equipment are as follows:

- Free weights, including dumbbells
- Machines, including Nautilus, Universal, Cybex Eagle, Paramount
- Apparatus, including Soloflex, Bullworker, Springs

Isokinetic strength training equipment controls positive contraction resistance only, making muscle soreness less likely. Such equipment includes Cybex, Keiser, and Hydrafitness machines.

Three strength routines are presented that you can easily teach to youth: a muscular endurance routine (using calisthenics), a basic weight training program, and a super circuit strength training program.

Calisthenic Training. Calisthenic training employs exercises in which the body weight and gravity supply the resistance. This routine works very well for developing muscular endurance but provides minimum absolute strength development unless the individual's strength is low to start with. One advantage of calisthenic training is that you don't need any equipment or apparatus. The calisthenic exercises for developing the major muscle groups are listed in table 6.3 (illustrated in figure 6.6).

An additional resource for calisthenic exercises is the following book:

The Weightless Workout (1991) by J. Robinson, published by Health for Life (Los Angeles)

Table 6.3	

Sample Calisthenic Exercise Sequence

Muscle group	Calisthenic exercise
1. Gastrocnemius (calf)	Calf raises
2. Quadriceps (front upper leg)	Three-quarter knee bends
3. Hamstrings (rear upper leg)	Assisted leg curls
4. Abdominals (stomach)	Sit-ups
5. Erector spinae (low back)	Back extensions (walrus)
6. Pectoralis major and deltoids (chest and shoulders)	Push-ups
7. Biceps (front upper arm)	Pull-ups or arm hangs
8. Triceps (rear upper arm)	Dips or chair dips

There are several steps to creating a calisthenic training routine.

1. The training routine should contain a variety of exercises that work all the major muscle groups. Order the exercises to work the larger muscles first so fatiguing a smaller muscle doesn't interfere with large muscles later in the routine. In addition, sequence the exercises to work alternate muscle groups or body parts. For example, for the arms, first do arm curls for arm flexors, then arm extensions for extensors.
2. Outline the routine on a form, such as the one shown in figure 6.7.
3. Determine the repetitions of each exercise that can be done in one minute.
4. Record the number of repetitions on the form.
5. Perform the routine three days a week.
6. During week one do one set of all exercises with the one-minute test score repetitions number. A set is one sequence of all the exercises.
7. During week two, divide the one-minute test score in half and do two sets of all exercises at that number of repetitions.
8. During week three, do three sets of all exercises at the half repetitions number.
9. During week four, maintain three sets but add one to two repetitions to each exercise every week thereafter.

Figure 6.7 shows a sample routine for the 13-year-old boy.

Weight Training. Weight training allows you to vary the resistance; thus, it is better than calisthenics for increasing absolute strength. All that is needed to develop a weight training program is access to free weights or weight machines. Use the exercises for the major muscle groups listed in table 6.4 (illustrated in figure 6.8), depending on the equipment available.

Additional resources for weight training exercises include the following:

Weight Training: Steps to Success (1992) by T. Baechle and B. Groves, Human Kinetics (Champaign, IL)

Getting Stronger (1986) by B. Perl, Shelter Publications (Bolinas, CA)

Standard safety procedures are very important in weight training.

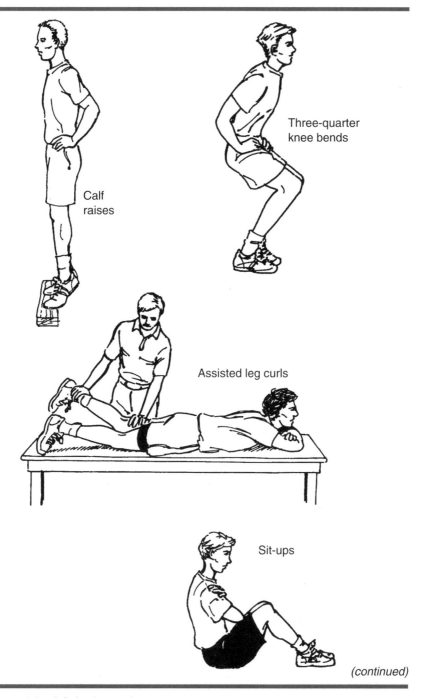

Calf
raises

Three-quarter
knee bends

Assisted leg curls

Sit-ups

(continued)

Figure 6.6 Calisthenic exercises.

Figure 6.6 *(continued)*

Calisthenic Strength Training Routine

Exercises

	Knee bends	Push-ups	Assisted leg curls	Sit-ups	Back extensions	Calf raises	Pull-ups	Dips
One-min reps	40	18	22	41	18	42	3	10
Half reps	20	9	11	20	9	21	2	5
Week 1								
Reps	40	18	22	41	18	42	3	10
Sets	1	1	1	1	1	1	1	1
Week 2								
Reps	20	9	11	20	9	21	2	5
Sets	2	2	2	2	2	2	2	2
Week 3								
Reps	20	9	11	20	9	21	2	5
Sets	3	3	3	3	3	3	3	3

(continued)

Figure 6.7 Completed calisthenic strength training routine.

	Knee bends	Push-ups	Assisted leg curls	Sit-ups	Back extensions	Calf raises	Pull-ups	Dips
Week 4								
Reps	22	10	12	22	10	23	3	6
Sets	3	3	3	3	3	3	3	3
Week 5								
Reps	23	11	13	23	11	25	4	7
Sets	3	3	3	3	3	3	3	3
Week 6								
Reps	24	12	14	25	13	27	5	9
Sets	3	3	3	3	3	3	3	3

Figure 6.7 (continued)

Table 6.4

Sample Weight Training Exercise Sequence

Muscle group	Free weights	Exercise machines
1. Gastrocnemius	Calf raises	Calf raises
2. Quadriceps	Squats	Leg press or leg extensions
3. Hamstrings	Assisted leg curls	Leg curls
4. Abdominals	Sit-ups	Abdominal curls
5. Pectoralis major and deltoids	Bench press	Chest press
6. Latissimus dorsi (upper back)	Rowing	Pull-downs
7. Deltoids	Military press	Shoulder press
8. Biceps	Arm curls	Arm curls
9. Triceps	Triceps extensions	Triceps extensions

- Precede a strength workout with calisthenics and stretching.
- Rest at least 15 seconds between performing each exercise.
- For each exercise practice the following:
  —Go from stretched to contracted position.
  —Go through the entire range of motion.
  —Control the speed of movement.
  —Practice proper form.
  —Use breath control, exhaling while contracting.
  —Avoid hyperventilating.
  —If using free weights, keep the weights close to the body.
  —Do not use free weights alone—use a spotter (an exercise partner who watches the person lifting and helps the person pick up and replace the weights in order to reduce the likelihood of injury).

There are several steps to designing a weight training routine.

1. As with calisthenic training, include in the weight training routine a variety of exercises that work all the major muscle groups and perform them in an order that works the larger muscles first.
2. Outline the routine on a form, such as the one shown in figure 6.9.

Figure 6.8 Weight training exercises.

Pull-downs

Military press

Arm curls

Triceps extensions

Figure 6.8 *(continued)*

3. Determine the one repetition maximum (1RM) for each exercise. The safest way to do this is to put a light weight on for each exercise (see table 6.5 for appropriate weights) and have the youth do as many repetitions as possible.

Based on the number of repetitions done in testing, you can make an estimate of the 1RM with table 6.6.

4. Calculate 60% of the 1RM weight and record it on the form.
5. Perform the routine three days a week.
6. Limit repetitions to 8 to 10 for each exercise.
7. During week one, do one set.
8. Week two, do two sets.
9. Week three, do three sets.
10. Weeks four and more, maintain three sets but add five pounds every four weeks to the training weight.

Figure 6.9 shows a sample routine for the 13-year-old boy.

Super Circuit Strength Training. It is possible to take a basic calisthenic or weight training strength routine and alter it slightly to maximize the development of both strength and cardiovascular endurance in the same workout. Super circuit training routines make three basic alterations.

- Instead of performing all three sets of an exercise then moving to another, you perform one set of each exercise in sequence then go back through the sequence two other times to complete the program.

Table 6.5	

Testing Weights for 1 RM Test Exercises

Exercise	Testing weight
Leg press or squat	1/2 the body weight
Bench press	1/3 the body weight
Leg curls	1/4 the body weight
Rowing or pull-downs	1/4 the body weight
Shoulder or military press	1/4 the body weight
Calf raises	1/2 the body weight
Arm curls	1/5 the body weight or 25 pounds
Triceps extensions	1/5 the body weight or 25 pounds

Weight Training Routine

Exercises

	Leg press (squat)	Bench press (chest press)	Leg curls	Rowing (pull-downs)	Military press (shoulder press)	Calf raises	Arm curls	Triceps extensions
1RM pounds	100	80	50	40	30	90	25	20
60% 1RM pounds	60	48	30	24	18	54	15	12
Week 1								
Reps	8	8	8	8	8	8	8	8
Sets	1	1	1	1	1	1	1	1
Week 2								
Reps	8	8	8	8	8	8	8	8
Sets	2	2	2	2	2	2	2	2
Week 3								
Reps	9	9	9	9	9	9	9	9
Sets	3	3	3	3	3	3	3	3

(continued)

Figure 6.9 Sample completed weight training routine.

	Leg press (squat)	Bench press (chest press)	Leg curls	Rowing (pull-downs)	Military press (shoulder press)	Calf raises	Arm curls	Triceps extensions
Week 4								
Reps	10	10	10	10	10	10	10	10
Sets	3	3	3	3	3	3	3	3
Week 5								
Reps	10	10	10	10	10	10	10	10
Sets	3	3	3	3	3	3	3	3
Week 6								
Reps	10	10	10	10	10	10	10	10
Sets	3	3	3	3	3	3	3	3

Figure 6.9 (continued)

Table 6.6

Estimates of 1RM Based on Test Results*

10RM	9RM	8RM	7RM	6RM	5RM	4RM	3RM	2RM	Estimated 1RM
16	17	18	19	20	21	22	23	24	25
22	23	24	25	26	26	27	28	29	30
26	27	28	29	30	31	32	33	34	35
30	31	32	33	34	35	36	37	38	40
35	36	37	38	39	40	41	42	43	45
38	39	40	41	43	44	45	46	48	50
41	43	44	45	47	48	50	51	52	55
45	47	48	50	51	53	54	56	57	60
49	50	52	54	56	57	59	60	62	65
53	54	56	58	60	61	63	65	67	70
56	58	60	62	64	65	68	69	71	75
60	62	64	66	68	70	72	74	76	80
64	66	68	70	72	74	77	79	81	85
68	79	72	74	77	79	81	83	86	90
71	74	76	78	81	83	86	88	90	95
75	78	80	83	85	88	90	93	96	100
79	81	84	87	89	92	95	97	100	105
83	85	88	91	94	96	99	102	105	110
86	89	92	95	98	101	104	106	109	115
90	93	96	99	102	105	108	111	114	120
94	97	100	103	106	108	113	116	119	125
96	101	104	107	111	114	117	120	124	130
101	105	108	111	115	118	122	125	128	135
105	109	112	116	119	123	126	130	133	140
109	112	116	120	123	127	131	134	138	145
113	116	120	124	128	131	135	139	143	150
116	120	124	128	132	136	140	143	147	155
120	124	128	132	136	140	144	148	152	160
124	128	132	136	140	144	149	153	157	165
128	132	136	140	145	148	153	157	162	170
131	135	140	144	149	153	158	162	166	175
135	140	144	149	153	158	162	167	171	180
139	143	148	153	157	162	167	170	176	185
143	147	152	157	162	166	171	176	181	190
146	151	156	161	166	171	176	180	185	195
150	156	160	165	170	175	180	185	190	200

*All RM measurements are in pounds.

Reprinted, by permission, from P.O. Davis, 1996, *Fitness coordinator's manual*, 12th ed. (Burtonsville, MD: ARA/Human Factors, Inc.).

- Instead of using 60% of maximum training weight, you use 40% of maximum training weight, increasing repetitions to 12 to 15.
- To get the aerobic training effect, the exerciser performs a 30-second aerobic activity (e.g., jogging, walking, jogging in place, or stationary cycling) between each exercise, allowing no rest between exercises.

Flexibility Training Guidelines

Exercise that stretches the muscles, ligaments, and tendons surrounding joints is what increases flexibility. Sitting and other static inactivity shortens muscles so they lose flexibility. Stretching is a key way to maintain flexibility. It can be used in four main ways:

- As part of the warm-up
- As a specific routine in itself
- As part of the cooldown
- As an activity any time you need to release muscle tension

The type of stretching used in flexibility training is static, or sustained, stretching. It involves one slow movement, holding the stretch for 20 to 30 seconds. There are six steps to performing a safe static stretch.

1. Move first into an easy stretch:
   - Hold 5 to 10 seconds—no bouncing.
   - When you feel a gentle pull, relax and hold.
2. Move into the developmental stretch:
   - Relax as you pull the muscle.
   - Wait for the tension to ease off.
   - Hold for an additional 20 to 30 seconds.
   - Slowly relax to normal.
3. Breathe slowly and rhythmically: Exhale as you stretch.
4. Gradually increase tempo if warming up; gradually decrease if cooling off.
5. Perform one to three repetitions of each exercise.
6. Think of a standard three-step process when stretching:
   - Slowly go into the stretch.

- Exhale as you stretch.
- Hold the stretch for 20 to 30 seconds.

A series of suggested standard stretching exercises are listed in table 6.7 (illustrated in figure 6.10).

Table 6.7

Sample Stretching Exercise Sequence

Muscle group	Stretching exercise
Gastrocnemius	Calf stretch
Hamstrings	Hamstrings stretch
Latissimus dorsi	Trunk bender
Quadriceps	Thigh stretch
Erector spinae	Knee pull
Quadriceps and groin	Sprinter stretch

A large variety of stretching exercises have been developed. A good resource that provides pictures of stretching exercises is Bob Anderson's book *Stretching*.

Stretching (1975) by R. Anderson, published by Robert A. Anderson (Fullerton, CA)

There are several steps to developing a flexibility routine.

1. Select the specific static stretching exercises that will also be used as part of the warm-up and cooldown and the total flexibility routine.
2. Use a form such as figure 6.11 to outline the routine.
3. Select when to do the exercises, either the time of day or as part of a total exercise routine.
4. Select the number of repetitions of each exercise (one to three).
5. Select the number of sets for doing the exercises (one to three).
6. Select the number of days for doing the exercises (three to seven).

Figure 6.11 shows a sample routine for the 13-year-old boy.

Calf stretch

Hamstrings stretch

Trunk bender

Thigh stretch

Knee pull

Sprinter stretch

Figure 6.10 Flexibility exercises.

Flexibility Routine

Exercises

	Calf stretch	Hamstring stretch	Trunk bender	Thigh stretch	Knee pull	Sprinter stretch
Days	4	4	4	4	4	4
Reps	2	2	2	2	2	2
Sets	2	2	2	2	2	2

Figure 6.11 Sample completed flexibility stretching routine.

Self-Control Skills Training Guidelines

The exercise planning element can teach youth how to increase fitness to reach a fitness goal. The next step is to teach them how to discipline themselves to follow their exercise programs. We can view developing self-control as a structured process that teaches youth to monitor and be accountable for their own behavior. To accomplish this difficult teaching task requires the definition of contingencies, the cues and rewards and punishments used to stay on course. Two methods have been found to be successful with at-risk youth: behavior contracting and maintaining an exercise log.

"Do" Steps for Self-Control Skills

The first "do" step consists of teaching a youth to contract with someone to stick with a program. The process is aimed at helping the youth define a behavior contract. The second "do" step is for the youth to maintain an exercise log, monitoring exercise behavior. By learning these two techniques, a youth begins to learn both how to supervise his or her own behavior and how to live up to an obligation.

Behavior Contracting

Behavior contracting is a process by which you secure an individual's commitment to follow a physical training program. It is an agreement between the person who is to follow a fitness program and a helper. It involves developing a written contract (not legally binding) that defines the contingencies that influence behavior. There are five steps to developing a contract:

1. Select a helper.
2. Define the exercise program.
3. Define cues.
4. Define consequences.
5. Write the contract.

Step 1: Select a Helper. The helper is the person who keeps the participant honest. It could be a brother or sister, friend, fellow participant, parent, teacher, or fitness leader. The helper must commit to working with the participant.

Step 2: Define the Exercise Program. By now, the exercise plan should have been already defined in terms of frequency, intensity, time, and type. What is left is to define the day-to-day exercise plan in terms of what, when, and where:

- What will be done
- When it will be done (time of day)
- Where it will be done (the place)

Step 3: Define Cues. Cues set the occasion for the desired behavior in different ways:

- The helper can use cues to encourage the individual to want to participate.
- The helper can use cues to separate the exercise session from other situations so that it is a focused time period.
- The helper can use cues as reminders to participate.

Here are some examples of cues:

- Choosing a set time for exercising
- Having a set place for exercising
- Having pleasant exercise surroundings
- Posting exercise posters
- Having the exercise routine posted so it's easy to see
- Having someone remind the individual to exercise (e.g., telephone calls)

The helper and the participant should discuss and mutually decide on the cues, based on what will "trigger" the individual and what is available.

Step 4: Define Consequences. We can view consequences in two ways: as rewards and as punishments. Rewards are much more successful in behavior contracting than punishments.

In using rewards, the most important part is to define a reward that is meaningful to the individual and can reasonably be provided. Use the following questions to help individualize a reward:

- What kinds of things would you like to have?
- What are your major interests?
- What are your hobbies?
- Who do you like to be with, and what do you like to do with them?
- What do you do for fun?
- What do you do to relax?
- What do you do to get away from it all?
- What makes you feel good?
- What would be a nice present to receive?
- What kinds of things are important to you?
- What would you do with an extra 10 dollars?
- What do you spend your money on each week?

We can define punishments as either having to do something you don't want to do or not being able to get a reward. Ask these questions to determine what might be a punishment for an individual:

- What would you hate to lose?
- Of the things you do every day, which would you hate to give up?

The helper and the participant should mutually agree on the appropriate reward and punishment.

Step 5: Write the Contract. Writing the contract involves filling in the blanks for the previous four steps and signing the contract form. Be sure to set a date four to eight weeks after the contract starts for reviewing performance and presenting the reward or punishment. Figure 6.12 is an example contract for the 13-year-old boy.

Monitoring Log

It is not enough to write out an exercise program and contract. Using an exercise monitoring log helps participants keep track of whether they are following their exercise programs and meeting the obligations of their behavior contracts. This process helps maintain self-discipline. Figure 6.13 shows the completed log for the 13-year-old boy.

Exercise Contract

I will (define the program in terms of activity, time, and place):

Run after school three times a week

I will get the help of: *John Smith*

My responsibilities (list cues, duties, and exercise requirements):

Bring running clothes to school and post the exercise routine on my locker.

Be at the gym at 4:00 p.m. Monday, Wednesday, and Friday.

Run my aerobic point distance and time.

My helper's responsibilities (list cues and monitoring duties):

Meet me at my locker at 3:30 p.m. to remind me to exercise.

Record my running time after exercising.

My reward (list reward and conditions for reward): *My helper gives me a Dr. Pepper every Friday I have done the running three days that week. I get a T-shirt if I stick with the program for eight weeks.*

My punishment (list punishment and conditions for punishment): *Give my helper a Dr. Pepper every Friday if I missed any days that week. I do not get a T-shirt if I miss more than three days over eight weeks.*

Date: *November 1, 1996*

Participant's signature: *Joe Doaks*

Helper's signature: *John Smith*

Figure 6.12 Sample completed contract form.

Adapted, by permission, from *Physical fitness specialist course*, 1993 (Dallas: The Cooper Institute for Aerobics Research).

Transferring Fitness Life Skills

The focus of the educational component is to teach youth the skills to design and maintain a personal fitness program. You can generalize the basic assessment, goal-setting, and planning processes to dealing with other health-related areas, such as nutrition and stress management. You can also address specific problem areas, such as substance abuse. The following examples are both modules from the First Choice Drug Demand Reduction fitness program to show how the same learning process can be applied to other areas.

Nutrition Life Skills

Three basic skills are presented here in the same framework as the fitness and exercise skills, with "do" steps. For this module, the objective is to teach youth to plan ahead to control what they eat. The focus of the content is as follows:

1. Checking yourself out. The "do" step is a dietary assessment of the types of foods eaten from the basic groups of the food pyramid:

   - Number of glasses of water
   - Servings of bread and other grains
   - Servings of meat and fish
   - Servings of vegetables
   - Servings of fruit
   - Servings from the milk group
   - Servings of fats, oils, and sweets

2. Setting a nutritional goal. The "do" step is setting daily serving goals from the food pyramid.
3. Designing a nutritional plan. The "do" step is to use a checklist to plan foods and serving sizes, listing what to eat during the day.

Substance Abuse Prevention Life Skills

Three basic skills to prevent substance abuse are presented here, following the same framework as the fitness skills with "do" steps. For this module, the objective is to teach youth how to respond to negative peer pressure to use drugs. The focus of the content is as follows.

1. Checking yourself out. The "do" step is a substance abuse self-assessment questionnaire, covering knowledge of the effects of

Exercise Monitoring Log

Date	Exercise performed
9/1	Walked 1.5 miles in 30 minutes
9/3	Walked 2.0 miles in 38 minutes
9/5	Walked and jogged 2.0 miles in 35 minutes
9/8	Walked and jogged 2.0 miles in 30 minutes
9/10	Jogged 2.0 miles in 25 minutes
9/12	Jogged 2.0 miles in 22 minutes
9/16	Jogged 2.5 miles in 30 minutes
9/18	Jogged 2.5 miles in 27 minutes
9/20	Jogged 3.0 miles in 32 minutes

Figure 6.13 Sample completed exercise monitoring log.

drugs and awareness of the pressures to use them as well as how to recognize those pressures.

2. Setting a substance abuse prevention goal. The "do" steps are using a decision-making matrix to assess the pros and cons of using a drug, then defining a specific prevention goal in specific situations. An example would be to not take a cigarette offered by friends at a ball game.

3. Designing a prevention plan. The "do" steps are defining ways to avoid or neutralize pressure situations by generating things to do and say and how to say them, then practicing them in role-play.

Conclusion

The ultimate objective of a physical training program is that participants will be able to maintain their own programs over time. A specific educational process designed to teach the skills to develop and maintain a personal program is required for this to occur. While we do not always have control over an individual's choices, we do have control over the learning process to ensure that the youth acquires the basic skills. For example, a youth may learn the skills at age 14 but not apply them seriously until age 17.

Sustaining a physical training program over time requires responsibility and self-discipline skills—traits too often lacking in at-risk youth. The self-assessment, goal-setting, planning, and self-control skills learned here are generalizable to the rest of their lives. The physical training domain gives youth a concrete example of how to apply these skills in meaningful ways, giving them vital life skills practice as they assume more of the responsibility and decision making for their own lives.

References

1. American Alliance for Health, Physical Education, Recreation and Dance. 1980. *Health-related physical fitness test manual.* Reston, VA: American Alliance for Health, Physical Education, Recreation and Dance.

2. Collingwood, T. 1995. *First choice: Taking charge workbook.* Richardson, TX: Fitness Intervention Technologies.

3. U.S. Department of the Interior. 1992. *Health and fitness guidelines NPS-57.* Washington, DC: National Park Service.

Chapter 7

Programming to Teach Values and Manage and Motivate Behavior

Most physical fitness programs consist of activities directed solely at increasing fitness levels or teaching fitness concepts and lifestyle habits. This approach is appropriate if the only program objectives are ones related to developing physical fitness. The thrust of this book, however, is on how to use physical training as a tool to teach other behaviors, such as life skills, and to reduce problem behaviors in at-risk youth. We can't assume that an exercise program will bring about these behaviors by osmosis; we must plan activities that will encourage the behavior changes we seek.

An overall concept that can be used to describe the other behaviors we want to teach is "values." For our purposes, we can define a value as a principle or belief in a trait that is important. A trait is an underlying factor that provides a consistent direction for behavior. But the only way that we can see a value is in terms of an individual's behavior, which is representative of the underlying value.

Deficits in values behaviors can be seen as major causes of the health-compromising lifestyle. Thus, teaching values is a legitimate part of the physical training program. Based on the experiences of program fitness leaders, at-risk youth commonly lack three values:

- Self-discipline—the ability to provide self-directed and planned effort toward reaching a goal
- Responsibility—the ability to meet obligations and follow rules
- Respect—the ability to show consideration of and value for oneself and for others

Concentrating on these three values does not mean that other values are not important or should not be emphasized or reinforced. Yet, these three values provide an example of how you might focus teaching efforts on values.

It is also clear from experience that a lack of behaviors representative of these three values is the major source for many class management problems. The most often asked question in fitness leader training courses is "How do I maintain control of these uncontrollable youth?" A common related question raised is "How do I motivate them to exercise?"

You can maintain control and motivation by focusing on values from the very beginning of the program. In other words, the way to control and motivate the behavior of at-risk youth is to teach them about certain values behaviors. This is not a new concept. An entire physical education curriculum can and has been based on values and behavioral expectations (2, 3).

Furthermore, designing an incentive system around participants practicing values behaviors can help teach values. You can use both individual and group incentives to motivate youth to practice not only the exercise habits but also values-based habits. Incentives can function as an initial step toward developing individual responsibility for behavior.

A fundamental program objective should be to provide a consistent values theme in all program activities. Specifically, we should help participants become more aware of the three values in the context of all physical training activities and help youth practice behaviors representative of the three values.

However, a formal teaching module on the three values is not what is required. Instead, a values theme should be integrated into all existing program activities. The values theme itself becomes the process by which you establish and maintain class control throughout a program.

In this chapter, guidelines will be provided for integrating the teaching of values into a physical training program and using values and incentives as tools for changing and motivating behavior. We'll discuss the six major program activities you can use to teach values through the physical training process:

- Initial participant orientation
- Incentives
- Physical exercise activities
- Educational activities
- Interactions with participants
- Group discussion

Guidelines for Initial Participant Orientation

The first meeting with participants sets the stage for what will occur throughout the program. That meeting provides the first opportunity to define the expectations and responsibilities for participants. The major guidelines for what should be covered are as follows:

- Give an overview of the objectives for and process of the physical training program.
- Give an overview of physical fitness and how maintaining a physical training program and healthy lifestyle affect fitness.
- Discuss behaviors that are examples of the three values as they relate to participating in the physical training.
- Provide concrete and specific "dos" and "don'ts" for program participation. You can present a code of conduct focusing on values behavior (see figure 7.1).
- Specify the positive and negative consequences for meeting your code of conduct.

Dos	Don'ts
Showing respect	
1. Encourage others	1. Curse
2. Respect others' property	2. Call people names
Showing self-discipline	
1. Control your anger	1. Talk when others are talking
2. Always be on time	2. Leave designated areas
Showing responsibility	
1. Enter and exit the building at designated places	1. Smoke
2. Complete homework assignments	2. Display gang signs, colors, or symbols

Figure 7.1 Suggested dos and don'ts for a code of conduct.

- If desired, employ a behavior contract similar to the type presented in chapter 6 to put the code of conduct expectations into operation. Have both the youth and the parent sign a contract promising to follow the code of conduct (see figure 7.2).

Guidelines for Incentives

Motivation to acquire a desired behavior is a factor that every program must try to build in as much as possible. Specific motivational strategies will be presented in chapter 8. One element of building motivation we'll examine here, however, is an incentive system. Building in an incentive plan is a key element of any physical training program. When most of us think of incentives, we think of rewards for following an exercise program and for meeting a fitness standard. Beyond this, however, you can use the same type of incentive system used to facilitate exercise behavior to reinforce values behavior. In fact, experience has shown that the motivational process intended to increase exercise habits is best accomplished by using an incentive plan that includes value behaviors as well as exercise behaviors. The two work as one to produce the desired results.

Incentive Factors

Consider six main factors when developing an incentive plan: the objective of the incentives, the timing, who receives the incentives, the requirements to receive the incentives, what the incentives are, and how they are awarded.

Objective of the Incentives. The more youth can earn incentives, the more they will participate fully. The objectives of the incentives are usually to reward either participation or performance. Address values by making values behaviors prerequisites for eligibility for incentives.

Incentive Timing. You must balance the timing of incentives between immediate reward and delay of gratification. More immediate gratification increases participation at first, when the more distant the gratification, the less the likelihood of involvement. Delay of gratification, however, is an important value to teach.

Consequently, incentives could be given daily, weekly, or at the end of the program. You could even use all three incentive times, perhaps creating a transition of incentives from daily to weekly to the end of the program as participants become more intrinsically motivated.

Incentive Beneficiaries. You can choose to grant incentives to either individuals or the group or both. Individual incentives are important to

Fitness Contract

I will: Follow the program's Code of Conduct.

My responsibilities are:

To show **self-discipline** by
—controlling my emotions,
—following directions, and
—being honest.

To show **responsibility** by
—making an effort at all times,
—being in class on time,
—taking part, and
—completing assignments.

To show **respect** by
—always trying to do better,
—encouraging others in class,
—helping the instructor, and
—not back-talking the instructor.

My instructor's responsibilities are:

To provide instruction and supervision.
To help me become more fit, more disciplined, more responsible, and more respectful.

My positive consequence or reward:

If I follow the Code of Conduct:

1. I will have the opportunity to select fitness activities.
2. I will have the opportunity to serve as a leader.
3. I will have the opportunity to participate in special events and field trips.

My negative consequence or punishment:

If I do not follow the Code of Conduct:

1. I will not be eligible for any of the incentives.
2. I may not be able to participate in class activities.
3. I will not be eligible to participate in any special activities.

Date: _____ Participant's signature:_____

Parent's signature: _____

Instructor's signature: _____

Figure 7.2 Sample completed fitness contract.
Adapted, by permission, from *Physical fitness specialist course*, 1993 (Dallas: The Cooper Institute for Aerobics Research).

teach individual responsibility. Group incentives use positive peer pressure to elicit participation and effort.

Requirements to Achieve the Incentives. The eligibility requirements should focus on behavior—both exercise and values behavior.

Requirements must focus on desired behavior. The desired behavior could be a combination of a code of conduct dos and don'ts and participation in specific class activities, such as completing an exercise circuit.

Requirements must be both specific and measurable. Specify your requirements in enough detail (ideally in specific behavioral terms) so that you do not have to use subjective judgment to determine whether someone meets a requirement or not. For example, if displaying a positive attitude is a requirement, you must break it down into specific behavioral terms, such as always follows directions, always arrives on time, does not back-talk, or encourages others.

Keep requirements consistent—no exceptions. Once you communicate the requirements, you must consistently include and exclude those eligible for the incentive, according to the requirements you set.

Choice of Incentives. The incentives chosen must be appealing to youth and be practical to provide. Examples are as follows:

- A "token" (fruit, pop)
- Recognition (applause, name posted on the wall)
- A recognition award (certificate)
- A recognition prize (T-shirt, sport ticket)
- Privileges (selecting activities or games, leading exercise activities, becoming eligible for a peer fitness leader training program)

An example of a privilege incentive is a group incentive activity called the Challenge Squad. It involves breaking the group down into equal teams or squads and following seven steps.

1. Have squads perform activities at a given station (calisthenics, stretching, and so on) for a set time period (e.g., 10 minutes).
2. Give squads points for starting on time and staying with the activity.
3. Subtract points when squads fight, otherwise disrupt, or goof off.
4. Declare the squad with the most points the winner.
5. Let the winning squad define a "challenge squad competition challenge course."

6. Have all squads participate in the challenge course.

7. The winning squad from the challenge course gets an immediate reward, such as each member receiving a can of pop.

Incentive Process. Communicate incentives and their requirements at the beginning of the program. The awarding of incentives could be automatic (i.e., if an individual meets the requirement, then the incentive is automatic), or you could state that meeting the requirements only meant they could participate in a lottery to get an incentive. In any case, specify guidelines for eligibility in detail. For example, everyone who completes an exercise circuit in a class is eligible for a lottery drawing to receive a bottle of pop at the end of class. Only one person receives the pop. Choose your incentives based on your resources.

Participation Incentives

The objective of the participation incentives is to reinforce four major behaviors:

- Following a code of conduct
- Practicing value behaviors
- Participating fully in all activities
- Completing of all homework assignments

Examples of incentive strategies include the following:

- Have youth fill in their own exercise logs. Set the number of activities that will determine eligibility for an incentive.
- Give participation points for good effort in a class. Although this involves a subjective call, it could be explained that each youth is being observed to see if he or she is making a good effort. A point chart could be posted, with a set number of points needed to earn an incentive.
- To be eligible for any incentive, require that the individual in question must have demonstrated values behavior (as defined by the dos and don'ts of the code of conduct).
- Present participation certificates for earning a certain number of attendance and participation points.
- Count the various participation requirements toward becoming eligible for a special event, such as a day at an amusement park.
- Organize all the participation incentives as team or squad requirements as well as individual requirements.

Performance Incentives

The objective of the performance incentives is to reinforce effort to increase fitness. Whereas the participation incentives should be aimed at all the youth, these incentives should be aimed only at those youth who demonstrate achievement. You can address both fitness levels and improvement of fitness levels. Examples of strategies include the following:

- Use a challenge board. Write the names on the board of people who earned the best scores on the pretest fitness test (one board for each age and sex). At the end of each class, allow any youth to challenge any record to get his or her name on the board. Base eligibility to challenge on having completed assignments, followed the code of conduct, practiced values behavior, and participated fully.
- Use certificates of achievement for meeting certain fitness standards (such as being above average on all tests).
- Use an achievement award (e.g., T-shirt) for improving the most on fitness tests.
- If desired, give improvement awards based on team or squad scores, giving all members of the group an award.

Sample Incentive Plan

Figure 7.3 shows a sample incentive plan for individuals and squads that covers activity participation, code of conduct behavior, and physical fitness improvement. The incentives are defined in terms of the following:

1. Timing for receiving the incentive
2. The incentive itself
3. The process for receiving the incentive
4. The process for establishing eligibility for the incentive

Guidelines for Teaching Values Through Physical Exercise Activities

Class management problems, which demonstrate a lack of values behaviors, tend to occur during three phases of an exercise class:

- Reporting and getting organized for class
- Periods when the fitness leader is talking, e.g., giving instructions, directions, roll call, and so on

Activity Participation and
Code of Conduct Behavior

Materials required: —Individual activity logs
                                   —Instructor point checklist
                                   —Activity poster for the exercise room for youth to write in their individual log information

General process: —Individual records personal activity log.
                                   —Leader records points for individuals and squads.

Timing	Incentive	Receiving the incentive	Eligibility for the incentive
Individual			
Daily	Can of pop	Lottery at the end of class	1. Meet activity effort 2. Have a good record of conduct
End of or during program	Peer leader program	1. Record daily in log 2. Record on activity poster	1. Average 5 activity points per week 2. Score 50% or higher on all fitness tests 3. Have a good record of conduct
End of cycle	Certificate and patch	Record in activity log	Earn 50 points, with each activity worth 1 point
During cycle	Special event participation	Record in activity log	1. Average 5 points per week 2. Have good record of conduct

Figure 7.3 Sample incentive plan.

Timing	Incentive	Receiving the incentive	Eligibility for the incentive

Squad

Timing	Incentive	Receiving the incentive	Eligibility for the incentive
Weekly	Select games and special events	All members do logs	Follow code of conduct

Physical Fitness Improvement

Materials required: —Challenge poster
                      —Fitness test record
General process: —Individual can challenge performance on a
                        fitness test any time.
                      —Leader records fitness test score.

Timing	Incentive	Receiving the incentive	Eligibility for the incentive
Any time	Name on challenge poster or board	Take fitness test	Have highest score for age and sex group
End of cycle	Certificate and patch, eligible for peer leader program	Take fitness test	Meet or exceed 50th percentile on all tests
End of cycle	Certificate and patch	Take fitness test	Meet or exceed 85th percentile on all tests
End of cycle	Certificate	Take fitness test	Demonstrate the largest percentage improvement for age and sex group

Figure 7.3   (continued)

- Periods when the participants are moving from one activity to another or moving into position to exercise

These periods are opportunities to stress the three values.

You can use five strategies to teach values during physical activity. First, the structure of class activities can set the scene for applying behavior representative of the values. For example:

- Set a standard class process so youth get used to the structure and know what you expect. This encourages responsibility and self-discipline.
- Break the group into squads or teams, assigning team leaders or captains, to provide the opportunity for teamwork and leadership experiences. This encourages respect and responsibility.

Second, you can assign homework at the end of the class, posting a homework assignment chart for youth to check off at the beginning of the next class period. This asks them to show responsibility and self-discipline. The following are some examples of homework activities:

- Follow an individual exercise routine at home.
- Try an activity you haven't done before.
- Go for an exercise run or walk for 15 minutes with a friend.
- Substitute a half hour of watching TV with doing a physical chore at home (washing clothes, taking out trash).

At the beginning of the next class, discuss the homework assignments in terms of following through on the assignment (demonstrating responsibility) and lessons learned from doing the homework assignment.

Third, present decision-making opportunities. Let the group select an activity for a day or allow the group to create an activity. This may foster responsibility.

Fourth, provide immediate feedback for doing something right and doing something wrong. Use the code of conduct as a reference point for clarifying expected behavior during exercise, focusing especially on examples of respect and meeting responsibilities.

You can offer feedback one-on-one or in front of the group. This depends on the nature of the behavior you want to provide feedback on and to what extent the feedback applies to everyone in the group. Negative behavior normally requires giving and getting feedback from a youth that focuses on "admit and commit," that is, admitting to doing the negative behavior and making a commitment statement to not do it again. For example, if a participant uses foul language, you could give the feedback in front of the group to highlight for the group (as well as the individual) what you expect and what you will not tolerate. You could also handle the same situation one-on-one by confronting the youth to force him or her to admit that the behavior is a violation of his or her word, which he or she gave by signing the code of conduct contract. Follow up by eliciting a recommitment to follow the rules.

Finally, seek opportunities to identify and reinforce positive values that participants display during exercise class. For example, you might state any of the following:

- Following directions in class shows responsibility.
- Encouraging others to make an effort shows respect.
- Controlling emotions and trying to do better shows self-discipline.

Guidelines for Teaching Values Through Educational Activities

The educational or life skill teaching modules are also opportunities to focus on a values theme. Certain modules easily lend themselves to highlighting values behavior. For example:

- The screening module can focus on self-respect and responsibility. You can use the screening process to launch discussions on the importance of health and how being concerned with your health shows self-respect. Reporting factual information about yourself (self-disclosure) regarding a health screening instrument can lead to discussions on being honest, reinforcing the need to be responsible to the objectives of the program.

- The assessment module can focus on self-discipline, responsibility, and respect for others. Instructions for taking the fitness tests can also cover the importance of not cheating, making an honest effort on the fitness tests, and recording the fitness scores accurately, all of which reflect responsibility and self-discipline. Asking participants to encourage each other while taking the tests provides an opportunity to show respect.

- The goal-setting module can focus on responsibility and self-discipline. While discussing the goal-setting process, you can present a theme of responsibility as an element of setting a goal. Then, you can focus the discussion on what it takes to reach a goal: self-discipline.

• The exercise planning modules can focus on self-discipline. You can lead a discussion on how self-discipline is required to follow the exercise plans to, in turn, reach a goal.

• The behavior control module can focus on respect, responsibility, and self-discipline as integrated values dependent on one another. You can lead a discussion about respect in terms of interacting with a helper in defining a contract and in honestly recording information in the exercise log. As an example of being responsible, you can present the signing of a behavior contract as an act of promising to meet an obligation, requiring self-discipline to follow through on the contract and the exercise plans.

Guidelines for Teaching Values Through Interactions With Participants

The daily interactions with participants offer many opportunities to focus on and discuss values. One way you can do this is by praising positive behavior that represents the practice of values. Examples include the following:

Self-discipline	Controlling emotions
	Following directions
	Being honest
Responsibility	Making an effort
	Following rules
	Completing assignments accurately
	Improving performance
Respect	Encouraging others
	Being helpful
	Demonstrating teamwork

Unfortunately, most of us do not praise people enough when they do something well or right. Often the only time a youth gets attention is when she does something wrong. Yet, praise is a powerful tool for reinforcing desired behavior. So look for opportunities to give praise. If you observe a desirable behavior, immediately praise the participant in front of the group. This gets everybody's attention as you give a positive stroke to the individual.

You can give praise in many ways. You might give an individual a simple pat on the back to say "good job" or talk one-on-one about the personal implications of performing the desired behavior. You might also pull the group together, give praise in front of the group, and discuss the implication of the desired behavior.

Another way to focus on values is to talk about negative behavior that does not reflect the values. Confront negative behavior in terms of not meeting the code of conduct. Employ a successive confrontational process in which, if each stage of the confrontation does not work, you go on to the next stage. This process involves successively clarifying behavior and expectations:

- Immediately focus on lapses of code of conduct behavior. State that the individual or group is not living up to their word or obligations.
- If the negative behavior persists, repeat and reintroduce this principle of the code of conduct: "*If* you meet the expectations, *then* you will get the reward. *If* you do *not* meet the expectations, *then* you will *not* get the reward." If necessary, explore the implications of not demonstrating the values of responsibility and respect for the group. Ask questions to elicit appropriate responses.
- If the disruption continues, have the youth sit out for a while, then allow him back into the group activity.

Finally, plan ahead for the kinds of reactions you may have to make to certain behaviors. Consistency is important. Each leader should make a list of potential reactions he or she would make to potential participant behaviors (see figure 7.4). There will be situations where serious violations of a code of conduct (such as bringing a weapon to class) could occur. In those situations the issue may not be so much one of discussion and interaction, but of swift and firm dismissal from the premises.

Praise	Confront	Ignore
Listening	Fighting	Talking out of turn
Following directions	Pushing	Inappropriate raising of hand to get attention
Hustling	Disrupting	Showing off
Being on time	Cursing	Snapping fingers

Figure 7.4 Sample list of potential leader reactions to participant behavior.

Guidelines for Group Discussion

Allow ample time for discussion during the course of the physical training program. The goal should be to provide time in each class meeting to discuss with the youth what they are learning and what the implications are for leading a healthy lifestyle. Then, focus the discussion on applying values and on avoiding unhealthy behavior, such as taking illegal drugs. Discussions can help you meet several objectives:

- To provide youth with feedback on their physical performances during the exercise class
- To give youth positive reinforcement for physical performance improvements
- To discuss what youth have learned from the physical activity in terms of respect, responsibility, and self-discipline values and self-assessment, goal setting, and planning life skills
- To discuss how what they've learned from physical activity applies to their personal problems at home, school, or in the community, especially for alleviating substance abuse and violence problems

Even though you can hold a discussion at any time and discussions should be very informal, the timing and discussion format are important.

Timing

In most cases, it is best to hold discussions after the physical activity, most of the time limiting duration to 10 to 15 minutes. For most groups, it's helpful to focus the discussion the first few sessions on what is occurring within the class. Over time, you can gradually transition to problem areas with more emotional content, such as drug abuse.

Discussion Format

If you have a set time period for holding discussions, you can apply a four-step format:

- Give and receive feedback.
- Focus on individual content or issues.
- Focus on themes.
- Summarize the discussion.

Give and Receive Feedback. Look for feedback related to physical activity, physical performance, and behavior representative of values.

Focus on Individual Content or Issues. Start by using an example from a group member on an event that occurred in or outside of class, holding this discussion at the time of the event or during the discussion period. Ask questions to direct the discussion, such as the following:

- How did that make you feel?
- What do you think the situation or behavior indicates?
- Why is it important to discuss this situation?

Focus on Themes. Look for a behavior to discuss from the angle of a personal example. Consider the following examples:

Values	Showing or not showing respect
	Showing or not showing responsibility
	Showing or not showing self-discipline
Life skills	Showing or not showing goal setting
	Showing or not showing planning
	Showing or not showing leadership
Personal results	Feeling or not feeling confident
	Feeling or not feeling respected
	Feeling or not feeling proud of accomplishments

Then generalize the themes from the class situations to other situations. For example, you could discuss the following:

School	Doing or not doing homework
	Following or not following school rules
Drug abuse	Handling or not handling peer pressure
	Avoiding or not avoiding high-risk situations

Summarize the Discussion. If possible, frame the discussion in terms of an action plan for the future. Specifically, follow a three-phase process (adapted from reference 1) during the discussion on individual themes to provide learning closure as shown here.

Exploration ⟶	Understanding ⟶	Action
Explore the material.	Focus on defining a goal to handle the situation.	Focus on a first step.

An example of a summary discussion is the following:

A youth lied about doing a homework assignment, saying he played basketball with another youth in the group after school. After discussing the situation with the group, a discussion summary highlighted the following.

Exploration ⟶	Understanding ⟶	Action
We explored what he did and why he did it. He felt embarrassed for not having done the homework. The boy didn't show respect for the other boy by asking him to lie and he did not meet his obligations.	We discussed and set goals, such as being honest and meeting obligations.	We defined a plan for ensuring homework was done. The boy made a contract with his friend to check with him daily to see if he had done his homework and promised to always be honest.

The discussion summary is for the entire group, not just the individual. Whether the discussion content is positive material (an event such as a participant showing respectful behavior) or negative material (an event such as being confronted to try drugs) the focus should be on how to learn from it to be able to do the positive behavior the next time.

Conclusion

A quality physical training program for at-risk youth should not only be directed at affecting exercise behavior but also at teaching, managing, and motivating value-based behavior. Teaching values behaviors should not be accomplished with a special module or activity, but rather by integrating values into your entire physical training program. The same holds for activities to manage, control, and motivate behavior. Therefore, integrate all aspects of your program to produce positive behavior change.

Values behavior and life skills are all associated with a lifestyle that is conducive to health enhancement. Ensure that achieving that healthy lifestyle is the overriding objective of your physical training program for at-risk youth.

References

1. Carkhuff, R.R., and B. Berenson. 1996. *Teaching as treatment*. Amherst, MA: Human Resource Development Press.

2. Hellison, D. 1978. *Beyond balls and bats: Alienated youth in the gym*. Reston, VA: American Alliance for Health, Physical Education, Recreation and Dance.

3. ———. 1985. *Goals and strategies for teaching physical education*. Champaign, IL: Human Kinetics.

Chapter 8

Support Programming

Support programming refers to other programs that can be provided to assist in the delivery of a physical training program. The support programs described here have been shown to help the physical training program better meet its objectives. The five major support programs are as follows:

- Parent programming
- Peer fitness leader programming
- Physical fitness council
- Special events
- Motivation programming

In some situations it may not be feasible to apply a particular support program or the options for employing a given program may be limited. In these cases, you must make a judgment call as to how necessary these support programs are for your physical training program. Experience has shown, however, that the more you can integrate these support programs with the basic physical training program, the higher the probability that you'll meet the needs of at-risk youth.

In this chapter, an overview of the elements of each support program is provided as well as guidelines to consider when incorporating each support program into the physical training program.

Parent Programming

Whenever possible, getting parents involved will enhance the ability of the program to impact the participating youth. The goal of parent programming is to get the parents to support the objectives and activities of the physical training program.

Parent Programming Elements

A variety of program elements can meet the goal of parent programming, including the following:

- A formal program briefing on the objectives, activities, and responsibilities of their child as a participant in the physical training program
- Opportunities for parents to be involved in the program as volunteers for duties such as transportation and supervision
- Formal parent training sessions

The specific opportunities for parent programming will depend on your site. Unfortunately, experience has shown that for most sites, only a minimal parent involvement is possible. Still, an effort should be made to provide as much parent programming as is feasible.

Parent Programming Guidelines

When planning parent programming, you first need to determine whether the parents of the youth in the program will be receptive to the idea, then decide what type of programming to offer and when.

Determining the Feasibility of Parent Programming. Many at-risk youth have disinterested or uninvolved parents. But before you reject the idea of parent programming, fully explore the possibility. Interview selected parents, especially those who have asked about the program, and network with social service and school staff working with the targeted youth.

Scheduling Parent Activities. The type of parent programming to be implemented will dictate the schedule of delivery. There are several general guidelines for implementing parent program elements.

For program briefing, send a written explanation of the program home (along with the informed consent form) or hold a briefing before the first class. Holding a briefing is the preferred option. You can give this parent briefing at the same time you hold the introductory class for youth. The briefing should be concise, leaving ample time for questions and answers. Present it in an informal atmosphere.

Parent involvement activities can vary. Brief parents about the activities in which they may serve as program volunteers. The following are suggestions for including parents:

- They can simply observe the classes and do mild exercise such as walking during the class period. *Caution*: Do not allow parents to participate in the exercise class, because they have not been medically screened.

- They can perform a role in regular classes, such as taking roll, organizing paperwork, and assisting in maintaining control.
- For special events, parents can assist with transportation and helping organize and control youth.

Specific parent training modules can be delivered in two different time frames: either all at one time during the first few class meetings or at different times throughout the program. The major factor determining which schedule is better is how much time parents are willing to give. It's hard to get a commitment from parents to attend a series of meetings, but providing too much material at one sitting may overwhelm them. Meetings must also be set around the parents' schedules, which usually means scheduling activities at night for short time periods and holding a minimal number of meetings.

Based on past experience, the following topics for parent modules work well:

- Choosing family fitness activities
- Behavior contracting with your child to support his or her participation in the program
- Personal health habit guidelines (activity, nutrition)
- An overview of community recreation and fitness resources

Modules should allow for parent participation. The following outlines the phases of a complete session:

- Overview of the topic
- Discussion of what they think is important about the topic
- Presentation of the basic information about the topic
- Parent "do" step in which they have to do some activity or learning exercise related to the module's content
- Summary of what was covered

Garnering parent support for a physical training program can help keep a youth involved, adding an additional "control" factor to the program, especially if a parent is actively involved in the program. In some instances the "parent" may not be the mother or father; it may have to be a grandparent, older brother or sister, or mentor. But the idea is—

whenever possible—to get a responsible adult or young adult to function in a supportive role.

Peer Fitness Leader Programming

A peer fitness leader program is based on a simple premise: Within the neighborhood, agency, or school, an informal peer leadership network will exist. The key is to direct that leadership toward constructive effort. A peer fitness leader program provides a leadership development experience that can support a physical training program by providing positive role models for participants. Many school and community agency programs have existing peer leader programs. The YMCA Leaders Club program and Students Against Drunk Driving (SADD) are good examples. You can link a peer fitness leader program with such efforts. Whether integrated with existing peer leader programs or as a separate entity, the program has a specific and narrow focus—physical fitness and physical activity programming.

The goal of a peer fitness leader program is to develop positive peer role models who can provide leadership to assist other youth in the physical training program and to provide a system to teach the value of community service.

Peer Fitness Leader Programming Elements

Peer fitness leader programs usually consist of a cross-section of volunteer youth and advisors. These advisors may be fitness leaders, teachers, volunteers from the neighborhood, or other youth service organization staff.

Advisors can take on the following roles. They can

- provide leadership training,
- provide program focus by giving needed direction on how to accomplish selected tasks,
- provide supervision,
- coordinate leaders' activities,
- give technical assistance to the peer fitness leaders, such as fitness assessments, goal setting, and exercise planning, and
- facilitate communication among youth, peer leaders, school and community leaders, and parents.

Peer fitness leaders can assume a variety of roles, including the following. Peer fitness leaders may

- serve as a squad or team leader to help supervise other youth in exercise classes,
- promote the physical training program,
- assist with fitness assessment and individual goal setting,
- assist with exercise instruction and leadership,
- coordinate program events,
- assist with individual exercise planning,
- serve as exercise partners and contract helpers for other youth, and
- participate in a community service project, such as cleaning up a park.

Surrounding these roles the peer fitness leader program consists of four basic elements: selection and instruction, assignments, establishing a peer leader organization, and a peer leader recognition system.

Peer Fitness Leader Programming Development Guidelines

To initiate a peer fitness leader program, first define the model, then make concrete plans.

Two basic models can be used for designing a peer fitness leadership program:

- Make the program an internal element limited to the physical training program. Leadership roles involve supporting the direct delivery of the program.
- Allow the program to expand out into the community, providing leadership opportunities beyond the physical training program. With this model, the leaders serve in community service roles, so you need to network with community or school agencies.

The planning process has eight major tasks:

1. Exploration of existing programs and resources that you might use in the peer fitness leader program, such as community programs (recreation, school, health, government), facilities (gyms, outdoor facilities), and people in the neighborhood.
2. Selection of potential advisors involving the recruiting of adults in the neighborhood.
3. Selection of target youth who have successfully completed the basic physical training program.

4. Definition of potential activities for year one, which involves deciding on the major roles and activities for the peer fitness leaders. Specifically define their responsibilities and tasks.

5. Scheduling of major dates for year one, which involves creating a schedule of major milestones for implementation to include the following:

   • Selecting advisors and youth
   • Scheduling advisor training
   • Scheduling peer fitness leader training
   • Scheduling major activities of the peer fitness leaders

6. Development of a peer fitness leader recognition system, which is a critical component of the program to get the youth involved. For many, the special recognition is the motivation to be a peer fitness leader, so some methods of recognition need to be determined:

   • Recognition awards
   • Visible symbols (patches, uniforms)
   • Yearly recognition event
   • Eliciting funding for recognition incentives

7. Selection of advisors on the basis of their willingness to volunteer their time and to undergo training.

8. Selection of peer fitness leaders through a formal application and selection process, including the following criteria:

   • Practices physical fitness
   • Has a positive image among peers (no substance abuse)
   • Has a positive leadership image among peers
   • Is committed to serve as a peer fitness leader and follow a code of conduct
   • Has successfully participated in the basic physical training program

As part of the selection process, you can employ another code of conduct behavior contract process to focus the commitment to be a peer fitness leader. Figure 8.1 shows an example of such a contract that has been successfully used with a peer fitness leader program called FITCORPS. The code of conduct is a modification of a code of ethics form developed for the YMCA Teen Leadership Program (1).

FITCORPS Code of Conduct

Being a peer fitness leader role model means following a code of conduct similar to the one you followed to participate in First Choice. But as a peer fitness leader you have a higher level of responsibility. You must uphold four areas of responsibility.

Responsibility to FITCORPS

- I will respect the privilege of being a member of FITCORPS.
- I will encourage others to join who would be an asset to and who would benefit from FITCORPS.
- I will perform my responsibilities as assigned.
- I will reflect the good influence of being a peer fitness leader through my own words and actions.
- I will always let my criticism of FITCORPS or First Choice be constructive, not destructive.

Responsibility to Other Peer Fitness Leaders

- I will avoid criticism of other members of FITCORPS except that which is formally presented by advisors.
- I will always report to my advisor any matters that involve the best interests of FITCORPS.
- I will always show respect to other peer fitness leaders and advisors.

Responsibility to My School and Community

- I will consider it my duty and privilege to help improve my school and community.
- I will maintain an attitude of respect and cooperation in dealing with teachers and school and community officials.
- I will observe all rules of the school and laws of the community, thereby encouraging other youth to do the same.
- My own standard of conduct will be higher than that expected by the school or the community.
- I will strive to be honest at all times.
- I will strive to do my best in my school work.

Responsibility to Myself

- I will take pride in who I am and what I stand for as a peer fitness leader.
- I will strive to maintain high levels of physical fitness.
- I will avoid the use of tobacco, alcohol, and other drugs.

_____   _____
Signature of peer fitness leader   Date

Figure 8.1 Sample code of conduct behavior contract.

Adapted from *YMCA teen leadership programs* with permission of the YMCA of the USA, 101 N. Wacker Drive, Chicago, IL 60606.

Peer Fitness Leader Programming Implementation and Supervision Guidelines

Training is necessary once the peer fitness leaders and advisors have been selected. Advisors also need to supervise the leaders throughout the year.

Advisor Training. Advisor training can be presented in one of two ways. If the advisors are staff who have received basic fitness leader training and are actively involved in delivering the physical training program, then additional training is not needed. Only a briefing to organize the peer fitness leader program is necessary.

But for those advisors who are not staff or who do not have a background in the field, you should give a detailed briefing, explaining fitness, the fitness program, and the peer fitness leader program.

Peer Fitness Leader Training. The peer fitness leader training is the first and most important event in developing the program. The training should be jointly conducted by program staff and advisors (if advisors are an additional group).

Ideally, the training should be conducted in one day. The schedule should be sequenced to alternate sitting in class and exercising so that participants are never sitting too long. The best setting is a gymnasium with a classroom (with overhead projector) for the cognitive material.

The training should be approximately eight hours long with content balanced among three major topics:

- Leadership and fitness principles
- Specific training on the skills, tasks, and roles expected of the youth
- Organizing the peer fitness leader group, electing a president of the group, and assigning responsibilities

A formal recognition graduation ceremony should be held after the training session. The peer fitness leaders should receive some type of symbolic and visible recognition for being a part of the program (T-shirt, pin, or the like). See figure 8.2 for an example of a one-day training schedule.

Supervision. The key to supervision of all activities is accountability between the peer fitness leaders and the advisors. The major supervision and implementation guidelines are as follows:

- Define and communicate to all a yearly schedule of activities.
- Internally define task assignments for all activities for accountability purposes.

8:00-8:15	Youth fitness program review
8:15-8:45	Peer fitness leader program overview
8:45-9:00	Commitment to the code of conduct
9:00-9:30	Leadership roles and activities
9:30-9:45	General leadership skills
9:45-11:45	Fitness skills: fitness assessment
11:45-1:00	Lunch
1:00-1:30	Fitness skills: goal setting
1:30-2:30	Fitness skills: exercise planning
2:30-3:00	Group exercise leadership
3:00-4:00	Peer fitness leader organization: selection of officers
4:00-4:30	Graduation

Figure 8.2 Sample peer fitness leader training session.

- Establish a chain of command structure between peer fitness leaders and advisors. The following is an example of a chain of command:

- Establish a monthly reporting system.
- Set a schedule of monthly meetings for the group.
- Once a year, hold some type of recognition event, such as a banquet.

A peer fitness leadership program extends the developmental ladder of experience for youth. Moreover, having more responsibility and getting recognition are two powerful motivators. A peer fitness leader program can channel a youth's initial effort toward responsible participation in a physical training program into another level of responsibility that focuses on service.

An additional expansion of the peer fitness leader concept is to provide a fitness or recreation career exploration component to the program. This has been successfully applied in several sites and has the following elements:

- Formal instruction on career exploration skills
- Formal instruction on fitness or recreation career areas
- Outside speakers in the fitness or recreation field
- Assignment to an internship site in a fitness or recreation program

This type of program is a logical extension of leadership in that the youth are expected to perform leadership functions at a higher level that moves them toward a more adult focus—the world of work. In some settings funding was available to pay a stipend for the youth to perform the internship, which was motivational.

Physical Fitness Council

Maximizing the use of community resources doesn't just happen. As with all aspects of implementing a program, a design for a plan of action is needed. Taking the following three steps can help to maximize use of community resources.

1. Awareness and education: This step involves both making the community aware of the physical training program and becoming aware of community resources.
2. Linkage: This step involves defining and implementing a working relationship between the community resources and the physical training program.
3. Communication and feedback: This step involves ongoing communication and feedback with the linked community resources.

The best way to accomplish these three steps is to establish a local physical fitness council. A physical fitness council is a group of interested parties from organizations, the community, or neighborhood who provide program support for the physical training program.

The goal of a council may be different in different settings, depending on the level of involvement the council members decide to commit to. Generally, the goal of the council should be to assist and support the efforts of the physical training program to involve all youth in constructive physical activity.

A number of community resources can be called upon to help meet physical training program objectives. They can be used in one of four ways:

- As sources for referrals of youth to the physical training program
- As sources of referrals of youth who need special assistance
- As sources for enhancing program services, providing people or services to deliver programming to youth
- As sources for generating support for the program

Some community resources that may make referrals include the following:

- Local schools
- Local youth recreation agencies (e.g., YMCA, Boys and Girls Clubs, recreation centers)
- Community mental health agencies
- Community substance abuse agencies
- Juvenile justice agencies (e.g., police youth divisions, juvenile court judges)
- Churches
- Mentor organizations
- Community service agencies (e.g., Big Brothers and Big Sisters)
- County health departments
- Hospitals
- Professional associations (e.g., American Dietetic Association)

Some community resources that can provide support include the following:

- Service clubs (e.g., Rotary, Lions)
- Neighborhood coalition groups
- Community committees or councils for substance abuse, mental health, juvenile justice
- Junior League
- Local school boards
- Churches

Council Elements

A physical fitness council can be a new entity or an existing community group that is willing to focus on youth fitness as an objective. It can serve four purposes:

- The council supports existing youth fitness and activity programs. This could involve the council taking on advocacy, networking, promotion, and fund-raising roles.
- The council coordinates efforts to get youth and their families involved in existing recreation, sport, and fitness programs, such as the physical training program.
- The council organizes a variety of special events, such as clinics and fun runs, possibly promoting, coordinating, and delivering special events.
- The council assists the peer fitness leader program. For example, they might provide promotional materials and expertise for planning special events to be run by peer fitness leaders.

A council may or may not assume the various responsibilities associated with the four purposes. Indeed, a council may function only as an input and feedback group to support physical training program efforts. Or it may accept many responsibilities, including members undergoing training so they may personally assist in the delivery of the program. The bottom line is this: Do not expect of the council what it cannot do. Instead, a major task in developing the council is to help them to decide their level of involvement.

Guidelines for Forming a Council

Once the decision is made to form a council, you must organize some initial preparation and training as well as create a plan to follow up.

Initial Preparation. Take three steps to start up the council.

1. Recruit the council members. This step should be coordinated with community contacts (e.g., Governor's Council on Fitness, housing authority, youth advocacy groups, school boards, and the like).
2. Hold a briefing meeting with prospective council members to tell them about the physical training program, including objectives, activities, and procedures, and how a physical fitness council can serve an important role in meeting the needs of the youth.
3. Determine what type of commitment the council wants to make. All involved must make an initial judgment and acknowledgment of the roles the council members are willing to play.

Council Training. No matter what roles a council is willing to accept, you must make sure they are briefed and given some level of training to perform their roles. For the council that will only function as an input and feedback group, the training should be limited to a detailed briefing on how the physical training program will be delivered and scheduled. Suggesting ways the council can recruit and support youth may be the only role they perform.

For the council that assumes more responsibilities and involvement, a formal training program could be provided in one or two sessions. The content of the training should focus on the following topics:

- Overview of the physical training program and the needs of the youth
- Definition of the council's roles and responsibilities
- Planning of a yearly schedule of council meetings and activities
- Assignment of responsibilities

Follow-Up. The follow-up activities represent the day-to-day functioning of a council. For the low level commitment council, make a schedule of monthly briefings that will keep all participants informed of each other's events and program activities. For the highly committed council, hold regular meetings weekly or biweekly and supervise and monitor their tasks.

Often the use of a physical fitness council depends on the nature of the physical training program setting. For example, a community-based program such as that at a YMCA may make considerable use of a council to sustain an ongoing community network. A self-contained school-based program, however, may not require linking with other community services.

Special Events

Special events are unique activities that can add some variety and excitement to the program. They can be viewed as adjuncts to the basic physical training program. By themselves, special events are not a program, but if you use them wisely, they can contribute greatly to meeting program objectives. Ultimately, the goal of special event programming should be to stimulate participant involvement.

Special Events Elements

A number of types of special events can be used for a variety of purposes, including the following:

- Culminating activities, such as a graduation ceremony
- Incentives or rewards for outstanding performance in the physical training, such as a field trip to a ball game
- Promotional "hooks" to get youth involved, such as offering a trip to an amusement park as part of the program's total activities
- Specific learning experiences for acquiring new skills, such as having youth participate in a ropes course or conducting a clinic on strength training
- Building program esprit de corps, group cohesion, or enthusiasm, such as holding a "Mini-Olympics"
- Promoting the program and building community support, such as holding a gala or open house
- Overcoming boredom, providing a break in the routine, or renewing program interest, such as holding a basketball tournament
- Focusing on the promotion of health, such as providing a blood pressure screening

Special Event Programming Guidelines

Only general guidelines can be defined because the specific nature of a special event dictates the specific tasks. However, the following six general guidelines can be applied. Provide ample time to complete all tasks.

- Doing initial planning (six months ahead). Determine the type of event as well as when and where it will be held. Ask the following questions:

  — What activities appeal to this group?

  — What are the budget constraints?

  — What resources are available?

- Coordinating the event date. The date may need to fit in with the organizational schedule, local sporting or fitness events, or national observances such as Fitness Month or "red ribbon" drug abuse week.

- Determining of a budget (four to six months ahead). Major budget areas to address are the following:

  — Personnel costs (e.g., referees, drivers)

  — Transportation

  — Food and beverages

  — Awards

—Equipment

—Promotional materials

- Ordering necessary items (e.g., trophies, clothing, and so on; four months ahead). You can identify many of these items as the budget is developed.
- Determining personnel needs (two to four months ahead). Decide on the types of roles and number of individuals required. Examples include the following:

—Event timers

—Drivers

—Referees

—Coaches

—Food and beverage servers

—Event promoters

—Event coordinators or supervisors

- Promoting the event (one to two months ahead). Planning for this includes developing strategies and carrying them out. Some types of promotion that can be used include the following:

—Brochures

—Posters

—News releases

—Radio or TV announcements or appearances

- Coordinating the event (one month ahead). At this point, all event tasks need to be identified and assigned. Examples include the following:

—Enrolling participants

—Setting up a facility

—Providing transportation

—Delivering the event

—Keeping records

Unfortunately, special events are often misused in that they are seen as the only elements of a program. But special events by themselves do not change behavior. When associated with an ongoing physical training program, however, they can be valuable strategies for helping to meet the program objectives.

Motivation Programming

Never assume that at-risk or any youth are naturally motivated to want to participate in physical training. In fact, their world often reinforces the reverse. Thus, a motivation program is a necessary component of a total program. The goal of motivation programming is to systematically control as many factors as possible that will motivate youth to exercise and stick with the physical training program.

A place to start in defining such factors is to examine what appears to be the difference between the youth who stick with a program and those who do not.

Why Youth Say They Drop Out

- Constant failure in competition
- No fun
- Poor choice of exercise activity
- Too much "drilling"
- Preexisting injury
- Mismatching youth at different levels
- Emotional stress to win
- Not getting in the game because of a lack of skills or lack of coaching attentiveness
- Receiving only negative feedback
- Not taught basic skills

Why Youth Say They Exercise

- To have fun
- To be with the group
- To get recognition
- To look good
- To be better in sports
- To have a place to go
- To try something new

A way of looking at the two groups of youth is to view it as a question of education and reinforcement of exercise as opposed to education and reinforcement to not exercise. It comes down to a question of programming. When we evaluate exercise programs in terms of their effect on motivating participants, several factors emerge as having a positive influence:

- Built-in family support
- Built-in peer support
- Provision of leadership
- Group activity support
- Appropriate exercise intensity
- Activity variety
- Convenience of location
- Leader modeling
- Feedback and reinforcement
- Flexible goals
- Individualized exercise plan
- Structure

Motivation Programming Elements

The elements of a motivation program can be categorized into three broad areas:

- The structure of the total program, which is designed to control as many factors as possible to provide reinforcement and support
- A structured incentive program or process (see chapter 7 for some guidelines regarding incentive strategies)
- Training of youths to improve self-control skills so they can sustain their own reinforcement and programs (see chapter 6)

Motivation Programming Guidelines

In previous chapters, guidelines were presented for using an incentive system and for teaching self-control methods. What is left is to define guidelines for structuring the basic physical training program for motivation purposes.

Five basic program strategies can be built into a physical training program, including the following:

- Environmental control strategies
- Social and interpersonal strategies
- External reward strategies
- Personal intrinsic strategies
- Activity stimulation

Not all strategies are appropriate for all youth or all physical training settings. These, however, represent a variety of ways to approach motivation for you to consider in the planning process as possible motivational strategies.

Environmental Control Strategies. These set the scene and context for participation. They provide a positive stimulus to the individual to participate. Examples include the following:

- Facilities that are accessible, clean, and aesthetically pleasing and have exercise equipment
- Communication vehicles such as exercise posters, information brochures, and bulletin boards that promote fitness and activity
- An organizational structure that provides proper supervision and ensures the program is run in a consistent and punctual manner
- Visible leaders who look and act as role models for fitness

Social and Interpersonal Strategies. These strategies utilize social reinforcers. Examples include the following:

- Group programming, including group exercise classes, excursions, and special events
- Peer and family programming, such as peer leader opportunities, buddy exercise systems, and family and parent activities
- Leadership techniques, such as verbal reinforcement and feedback

External Reward Strategies. These are incentives and rewards for participation that give recognition. Examples include the following:

- Symbolic recognition, such as fitness awards, T-shirts, and patches
- Material rewards, such as prizes, money, or special privileges
- Prerequisites for inclusion in a special group, such as peer fitness leaders

Personal Intrinsic Strategies. These strategies appeal to the individual's personal health and fitness situation. Examples include the following:

- Pre-post fitness assessments for feedback on personal performance
- Education to provide the information for improving fitness and health and for personalizing exercise to meet individual needs

Activity Stimulation Strategies. These are methods to renew interest in participation and to prevent staleness. Examples include the following:

- Planning for program variety by creating activity tournaments, sport clinics, and different types of group exercise classes
- Providing special events such as fun runs, Mini-Olympics, and field trips

General Guidelines. Whatever motivational strategies you use, the general guidelines for their application are as follows:

- Decide on the structure for how the various strategies will be used before implementing the physical training program.
- Apply all strategies in a consistent manner.
- Continue to seek new and innovative ways to build motivation into the total program.

Many of these strategies are built into the programming guidelines defined in previous chapters. In many respects everything that is done in a physical training program could be classified as being either motivating or not motivating. The issue isn't so much one of having a motivation program as it is of ensuring that the program itself is motivating.

Conclusion

The various support programs can enhance the delivery of a physical training program in order to accomplish its objectives. The more of these support programs that you can incorporate into your physical training program, the higher the probability of your program's success. This is especially the case with at-risk youth. One program alone often has little effect. Therefore, the more services that can be brought to bear to support behavior change—especially exercise behavior—the greater the impact of the program.

But only you and your organization can determine the feasibility of applying the various support programs to your setting. Logistics and resources will often dictate how applicable each support program is. Whenever possible, however, add these program areas to the services you already deliver.

References

1. Zoller, M. 1992. *YMCA teen leadership program.* Champaign, IL: Human Kinetics.

Organizational Issues

Part III addresses the organizational issues related to implementing a physical training program, based on the learnings described in part I.

Chapter 9 provides guidelines for developing the leadership necessary to deliver an effective physical training program. These include guidelines for defining staffing patterns, leadership roles, leader competencies, leader selection and training, and ongoing leader development.

Chapter 10 covers guidelines for coordinating and administering a physical training program. First, guidelines are discussed for creating the program structure, defining the target population, linking with other organizations, and scheduling programs. Then specific delivery guidelines for program promotion, facility management, record keeping, program evaluation, and program supervision and coordination are presented.

Chapter 9

Leadership

After training over 10,000 physical fitness leaders, I am convinced that leadership is the key element for any physical training program. Indeed, for any physical training program to meet its goals, it must have well-trained fitness leaders. Unfortunately, the development and delivery of physical training programs does not always place enough emphasis on the leadership component.

In this chapter, guidelines for fitness leadership development will be provided, covering the following areas:

- Staffing patterns
- Leadership roles
- Fitness leader competencies
- Fitness leader preparation
- Leadership development

Staffing Patterns

Part of implementing a physical training program is establishing a staffing pattern. One way of defining that pattern is to break the leadership component into two parts: delivery and support. The delivery leaders are those staff responsible for the day-to-day supervision and implementation of the physical training program. Support leaders are the administrators and supervisors who play an important supportive role in the application of the fitness program. The different roles reflect the major program tasks:

- Delivery tasks include program design and delivery of the major components of a fitness program (screening, assessment, teaching exercise classes), scheduling, coordination, and fitness program supervision.
- Support tasks include policy and budget development and communication.

In many organizations serving at-risk youth, personnel in an existing organizational structure may arrange the delivery and support tasks. For example, schools, recreation centers, and community agencies, such as YMCAs and YWCAs and Boys and Girls Clubs, have certain staff dedicated to exercise programs. Treatment and correctional centers often have recreational therapists. In other settings, an existing staff member may be asked to perform physical training program leadership as an additional job responsibility. Whichever structure is defined, the specific roles and responsibilities of each staff position must be made clear.

Leadership Roles

How well the roles of delivery and support leaders are defined and how well staff members fulfill these roles will determine others' perception of the program and, ultimately, its effectiveness. Both fitness leaders and administrators have key roles in the program.

Fitness Leaders

Fitness leaders must play three major roles to be effective:

- **Role model.** The fitness leader must lead by example. He or she need not be a bodybuilder, but must be a visible example of the healthy and active lifestyle.
- **Program manager.** The fitness leader must be organized, implementing a well-coordinated and adequately scheduled program.
- **Behavior change agent.** Getting youth, especially at-risk youth, to exercise requires changing behavior. Thus, the fitness leader must know how to help youth change habits, using program elements such as assessment and goal setting.

Experience providing fitness leadership training has helped to clarify and expand the definitions of these basic roles, illuminating eight specific roles that a fitness leader must fulfill to provide an effective physical training program. For each role, levels of responsibility will differ, based on the unique organizational structure. The matrix in table 9.1 can aid in defining the specific roles of fitness staff.

Program Administrators

It's not enough to have well-trained fitness leaders. A successful physical training program requires administrative support as well. Like the fitness leaders, program administrators must assume corresponding supportive leadership functions. Two basic support roles are defined in table 9.2.

Table 9.1

Fitness Leader Roles

LEVEL OF ROLE RESPONSIBILITY

Role	Low	Medium	High
1. Program manager (planner)	Coordinates individual participants' programs, schedules	Gathers program input and sets program objectives	Handles program budget and facility, staffing
2. Assessor (tester)	Obtains histories, interviews	Performs field fitness tests	Conducts stress tests, blood studies
3. Counselor (coach)	Communicates regularly with participants	Assists participants in developing goals	Is involved in formal problem solving
4. Fitness program planner	Outlines exercise principles	Develops written exercise plans	Develops ongoing exercise and nutrition plans
5. Participant supervisor	Monitors participants	Monitors and gives feedback to participants	Provides fitness reevaluation, feedback, and program redesign
6. Exercise leader	Leads by example	Develops and leads group classes	Develops and leads scripted lesson plans for classes
7. Educator	Orients participants	Teaches proper exercise techniques	Develops curriculum and provides formal educational programs
8. Motivator	Sets example, gives verbal encouragement	Develops recognition system and special events	Provides behavior modification programs

Table 9.2

Program Administrator Roles

LEVEL OF ROLE RESPONSIBILITY

Role	Low	Medium	High
1. Policy maker	Defines positive policy about the program	Models fitness, facilitates the program	Dedicates budget
2. Individual supervisor	Communicates and supports policy	Models fitness, participates in program	Schedules activities, provides reinforcement

Fitness Leader Competencies

In order to carry out the roles they have been assigned, fitness leaders must have certain competencies. Experience in training and supervising fitness leaders over the years has helped me define the skills and knowledge competencies required to perform effectively as a fitness leader. Based upon that experience, the following competencies are necessary for fitness leaders to function effectively:

Skills

- Health and medical screening
- Fitness assessment skills
  - Cardiovascular endurance
  - Strength
  - Flexibility
  - Body composition
- Goal-setting techniques
- Individual exercise planning
  - Cardiovascular endurance
  - Strength
  - Flexibility
  - Weight control
- Group exercise leadership

- Motivation strategies
- Interpersonal skills
- CPR and first aid skills

Knowledge

- The elements of physical fitness and wellness
- The justification of fitness for physical and psychological health, risk reduction, and reduction of problem behavior
- Anatomy and kinesiology
- Exercise physiology
- Nutrition principles
- Principles of learning and behavior change
- Safety programming
- Program coordination

It's important to recognize that the degree to which a fitness leader possesses these competencies determines the success or failure of the program. Indeed, how the fitness leader applies these skills and knowledge directly relates to how well youth will respond to the program. This is what leadership is all about—especially when leading exercise classes.

The most critical skills are those necessary for leading exercise classes. The leader must be dynamic, and an acronym that captures the dynamic application of those skills is FIRE. This acronym applies to all fitness leadership activities, especially, however, to the day-to-day interactions with participants.

- Feedback
- Instruction
- Reinforcement
- Enthusiasm

• **Feedback.** This includes constantly giving participants feedback on their performances, behavior, and attitudes and using that information to stimulate questions and answers. For example, a fitness leader might mention to a participant that he noticed the participant is doing more sit-ups, asking how that makes him or her feel.

• **Instruction.** Instruction means always looking for opportunities during class to teach about fitness as well as about values and responsibilities. For example, a fitness leader might teach a youth the correct form for running, explaining how the information will make it easier to meet the homework assignment for running.

- **Reinforcement.** This means always looking for opportunities to reward participants for their performance, effort, and appropriate behavior. For example, a fitness leader might allow a youth to lead an exercise class because he or she encouraged another participant to stick with an exercise.
- **Enthusiasm.** Enthusiasm means always delivering the class with high energy. By keeping his or her attitude positive, the leader shows that he or she values the program. For example, a fitness leader should always exercise with participants.

Fitness Leader Preparation

The ideal candidate for a fitness leader position is an individual who has an academic degree in the field (physical education, kinesiology, health education) and is certified by an existing fitness leader program. As is often the case, however, your program may not have the funding to finance such a position. If this is true, the agency will probably have to accept the challenge of preparing the fitness leader. Three areas require attention when preparing fitness leaders: selection, training, and certification.

Selection Guidelines

Candidates for fitness leader positions, whether full time or part time, should undergo a selection process. Avoid the following two extremes when screening candidates: a knowledgeable person who understands fitness but does not live a fit lifestyle or the fit person who is perceived as a fitness fanatic but doesn't know how to deal with youth. Neither extreme will work well. Over the years, the following basic criteria have emerged as selection guidelines:

- The candidate should be a role model who exercises regularly, does not smoke, and scores above average on fitness tests.
- The applicant should have good interpersonal skills and enjoy dealing with people, especially with youth.
- The applicant should have a commitment to the role as demonstrated by being a self-starter and an active learner.

Training Guidelines

Training is critical to ensure that the fitness leaders have the necessary skills and competencies; thus, the selection of the training program to prepare fitness leaders is an important administrative decision. Unfortunately, the fitness field is inundated with pseudo-experts. Credibility is an important issue, and you must be sure the training organization and its instructors have a good reputation. Fitness leaders must be validly trained from both a liability and an accountability perspective.

One of the problems with many organizations that provide fitness leader training is that they tend to be at one of two extremes. Either they are academic organizations with little practical expertise in dealing with at-risk youth, or they have experience in training youth workers but do not have any fitness expertise. Consequently, a selection process is recommended to choose the most appropriate training program. Look for the following criteria when selecting a training program:

- The training faculty should have educational credentials in physical education, exercise physiology, or other fitness-related fields.
- The training faculty should have practical experience in running physical training programs for at-risk youth.
- The training program should have experience in providing the training course specifically for organizations serving at-risk youth.
- The training program should focus on the leader competencies that have been defined.

Some organizations that meet these criteria are Fitness Intervention Technologies, some YMCAs, and the Cooper Institute for Aerobics Research.

Fitness Intervention Technologies, 2505 Canyon Creek, Richardson, Texas 75080, 972-231-8866

Cooper Institute for Aerobics Research, 12330 Preston Road, Dallas, Texas 75201, 972-701-8001

If your organization is large enough to have a full-time fitness program director, that individual should receive advanced training specifically aimed at developing higher levels of fitness expertise. The American College of Sports Medicine is recommended, which has valid courses in this area.

American College of Sports Medicine, P.O. Box 1440, Indianapolis, Indiana 46206-1440, 317-637-9200

Certification Guidelines

Certification is a process by which fitness leaders who have undergone training take and pass a written and practical test to demonstrate mastery of what was taught in the training. As with the training courses that are available in fitness, some questionable certification programs exist. Make sure that the training and certification programs are linked so that, if the staff are trained on the skills and tasks defined for their expected roles, the certification ensures that they have mastered that training. Thus, the fitness leader training program should have a validated testing program to measure leaders' mastery of the skill and knowledge objectives. Both written and practical skill certification are necessary. The training programs recommended all meet these criteria.

Leadership Development

The development of program leadership does not end with the completion of training and certification. Ongoing systems need to be in place to support the sustained learning of the fitness leaders and to maintain administrative support.

Fitness Leader Development Guidelines

An ongoing system for upgraded and advanced training for fitness leaders is essential. A yearly in-service is recommended, the content of which should be based on an assessment of fitness staff training needs. In addition, many fitness certifications require ongoing education to maintain the certification. These educational requirements can be met by the organization's commitment to providing ongoing training for fitness leaders.

If the agency or organization does not have the educational capability, many professional associations such as the YMCA and the American College of Sports Medicine offer periodic seminars for fitness professionals. If possible, the organization should provide funding for memberships in professional organizations and for attendance at fitness-related educational seminars.

Administrators' Leadership Development Guidelines

Administrators' leadership can be sustained in two main ways. First, your program can provide special fitness assessments and programs specifically for administrative staff. These programs should be aimed at assisting administrators, as individuals, with their personal fitness programs. This is helpful because administrators' personal commitments to fitness will be a highly visible way to show support for the program.

Second, periodic status reports should be issued by the fitness leader regarding the physical training program. Documenting the benefits of the program through a program evaluation assists administrators in building support for their policy and budget development for the program. (See chapter 10 for more on program evaluation.)

Conclusion

Fitness leadership determines the success or failure of any physical training program. As a consequence, you must select, train, and certify fitness leaders in a systematic manner to ensure success. Unfortunately, however, staff training and development is a low priority in many organizations serving at-risk youth. Don't settle for this in your program! Refocus priorities to make staff development services more effective. Remember, equipment and facilities do not change behavior—people do.

Program administrators are important as well. If they do not understand or promote the physical training program, the program is likely to be underfunded and ineffective. So plan to do training with administrators also.

Chapter 10

Program Coordination and Administration

A simplified way of viewing coordination and administrative factors is that they are the components that link the staff elements to the program elements so that the organization can deliver a physical training program effectively. From an applied perspective, the goal is to organize, integrate, and focus all those staff and program resources on meeting the needs of the at-risk youth you serve. A variety of organizational factors require attention; we can classify them broadly as planning and delivery elements. In this chapter, an overview of these elements will be provided with guidelines for addressing them.

Planning Elements

An acronym that summarizes the importance of the planning function is PPPP. It can stand for either "Poor Planning leads to Poor Performance" or "Proper Planning leads to Premier Performance." Address the following planning areas before actually implementing your physical training program:

- Organizational structure
- Program site selection
- Target population definition
- Linkages with other organizations
- Program scheduling
- Program sequencing

Organizational Structure Guidelines

Most applications of a physical training program for at-risk youth will occur within an organizational structure. A school, a recreation center, a community agency, a treatment or correctional center, or similar organization will be sponsoring or delivering the program as a service area for the organization. To avoid confusion and discord, ensure that a well-defined chain of command exists regardless of the nature or structure of the organization. Those responsible for delivering the physical training program must have a line of accountability through the sponsoring organization.

During planning, define the chain of command so that all know who is accountable to whom. A well-defined structure is one that describes responsibilities along the lines of function, including who delivers each task, who is responsible for supporting the delivery of tasks, and who is responsible for supervising the implementation of tasks.

Program Site Selection Guidelines

You may have a number of site options to deliver a physical training program. A single room or gymnasium space may be all that is available. Consider the possibility of using a city recreation center, YMCA, YWCA, Boys or Girls Club, school, church hall, or National Guard armory. To select an appropriate site, adhere to several guidelines:

• **Location.** Take into consideration participant convenience to get to the site. The site will not be used if participants don't have easy access. Distance, available time periods for use, and the availability of transportation are important factors. Safety is important as well. For example, a site will not be used by youth if it means the youth must cross a gang boundary.

• **Site space.** The exercise space should be configured to allow separate space for flexibility and stretching, strength training, and cardiovascular endurance training. If the site has room for exercise classes, the class space should be large enough to allow at least 36 square feet per participant.

• **Equipment.** A site that has a variety of equipment will offer more program options. Having equipment, however, is the least important selection factor. Remember, a physical training program does not have to have equipment to be effective.

• **Cost.** The selection of a site must also take into account any cost in using that site, such as rent or utility or user fees.

• **Availability.** The schedule for delivering the program in terms of days, hours, and weeks will have to match the times the facility is available. Keep in mind that most successful programs last 8 to 12 weeks.

Target Population Definition Guidelines

It is important to define the specific target population that the physical training program will be aimed at. Having a well-defined group of youth can help you promote and schedule your program. Consider the following demographics:

- Age and sex composition of the group
- Specific neighborhood the youth live in
- Specific school or grade they attend
- Specific problem area, if defined, such as drug abuse or dropping out of school
- Specific program they may be involved in, such as probation, counseling, or a YMCA class

In some settings, a program may focus on a particular group, such as youth on probation or youth from a specific school. In other settings, it may be on a first come, first served basis. But regardless of your situation, it is important to have a sense of who it is you want to serve.

Guidelines for Linking With Other Organizations

The nature of the setting for a physical training program will dictate the extent that linkages with other organizations are required. These linkages may be internal or external.

When a physical training program is just one program offering of a larger organization delivery system such as a YMCA, the linkage is internal. In such a situation be sure that you maintain adequate communication with the parent organization. Moreover, work to integrate the time during which the physical training program is conducted with the schedule of other services. This prevents internal confusion over use of resources and allows participants to avail themselves of other services as well.

Working with external organizations to deliver a physical training program that is integrated with other services demands a sensitivity to "turf" issues. The more you can present and apply the physical training program as a complementary service that helps fill a void, the better. Adequate communication and timing are as important, if not more so, as in the case of the internal organization.

Regardless of setting, an important consideration is to define the process, in detail, by which prospective youth are to be referred into or out of the physical training program by linking organizations. For example, a county juvenile justice probation program may refer a youth to a physical training program offered through a YMCA. It's important to define very specific procedures for that type of relationship. For example, procedures for defining the type of juvenile offender eligible for the program must be established by the court. If completing the program is a condition of probation, the court must define those requirements and establish security measures for all record keeping. In such a case the YMCA might restrict the exercise program to include only youth on probation.

Program Scheduling Guidelines

The scheduling of a physical training program is highly unique to the specific setting. Generally, a physical training program is scheduled in two ways: either in cycles of a set number of meetings over a certain number of weeks or as an open enrollment and exit program that's continuous.

Cycles have a set beginning and ending date with a particular group of youth enrolled. A new group enrolls at the end of each cycle. The following are examples that have been employed successfully:

- A semester-long physical education class that meets for four one-hour sessions every week for 16 weeks
- An after-school fitness club that meets one night a week for three hours for a semester
- A 12-week class offered at a recreation center or Boys and Girls Club that meets three evenings a week for two hours each session

Programs using cycles tend to be 12 to 16 weeks in duration. Most community-based sites offer a program three days a week for approximately one to two hours a session, while most institutional or school-based programs offer a program daily for approximately an hour.

In an open enrollment and exit program, the program is continuous with a set number of meetings per week or month. Participants come and go at any time. An example of such a program is a substance abuse treatment facility program or correctional agency in which the youth enter and exit the facility at different times. The classes are offered for one hour either three or five times a week.

To define the program sequence and determine your schedule, first decide whether you want to use cycles or have open enrollment and exit. If you choose cycles, then determine the number of weeks per cycle, the number of sessions, and the length of each session. Finish by deciding on the number of cycles per year.

Program Sequencing Guidelines

Program sequencing is determining the program's elements or activities and their order in program sessions. First, decide which activities to use, including support activities such as parent programming or special events; then sequence the activities; and, finally, write down a minute-by-minute schedule for each session. Examples of program sequencing include:

Two-Hour Class

30 minutes exercise

20 minutes education

10 minutes discussion

40 minutes exercise

10 minutes education

10 minutes discussion

One-Hour Class

35 minutes exercise

15 minutes education

10 minutes discussion

Use the form shown in figure 10.1 to outline each class.

The sequence for ordering class sessions within a cycle varies, depending on the number of weeks the cycle takes and the time allotted for each session. Figure 10.2 shows an example of a 10-week cycle with three sessions a week.

Delivery Elements

Delivery elements are those organizational functions that are necessary on a day-to-day basis, including the following:

- Program promotion
- Facility management
- Record keeping
- Program evaluation
- Supervision and coordination

Session 1	Session 2	Session 3
Exercise	Exercise	Exercise
Education modules	Education modules	Education modules
Other activities	Other activities	Other activities

Figure 10.1 Sample class elements form.

Program Promotion Guidelines

Promotion is informing others of the physical training program so that participation and support expands. Three major goals for promotion are to create an awareness of the program and its benefits, to motivate youth and parents to participate, and to sustain program support within the organization and community.

Everything done within the program and the organization, at least on one level, is promotion. Indeed, a quality program promotes itself. If we look at it this way, we can view everyone involved in the project as a promoter and any time as the time to promote. Yet, meeting promotion objectives requires planning, contacting people, and varying promotional strategies.

	Session 1	Session 2	Session 3
Week 1			
Exercise	Warm-up, cooldown (learning exercises) Relays	Warm-up, cooldown (learning exercises)	Warm-up, cooldown (learning exercises) Fitness assessment
Education	Program introduction	Health screening	Fitness assessment
Other	Behavior contract for code of conduct	Fill in health history	Fill in fitness assessment
Week 2			
Exercise	Warm-up, cooldown (learning exercises) Fitness assessment	Continuous rhythmical exercise Basketball	Continuous rhythmical exercise Basketball
Education	Fitness assessment	Fitness profiling	Fitness goal setting
Other	Fill in fitness assessment	Compare scores to norms	Set goals
Week 3			
Exercise	Continuous rhythmical exercise Relays	Jogging Basketball	Continuous rhythmical exercise
Education	Aerobic training	Aerobic points training	Calisthenic training
Other	Monitoring heart rate Use of heart rate training	Fill in aerobic points chart	Calisthenic 1-minute exercise testing
Week 4			
Exercise	Calisthenic super circuit	Calisthenic super circuit	Sports and games
Education	Calisthenic training	Calisthenic super circuit	None
Other	Fill in calisthenic training form	Fill in calisthenic super circuit form	None
Week 5			
Exercise	Calisthenic super circuit	Calisthenic super circuit	Weight training super circuit
Education	Weight training	Weight training	Weight training super circuit
Other	1 RM testing	Fill in weight training form	Fill in super circuit weight training form

Figure 10.2 Sample 10-week cycle sequence.   *(continued)*

	Session 1	Session 2	Session 3
Week 6			
Exercise	Weight training super circuit Stretching circuit	Continuous rhythmical exercise	Weight training super circuit
Education	Flexibility training	Monitoring and contracting	None
Other	Fill in flexibility form	Fill in behavior contract	None
Week 7			
Exercise	Youths' choice	Basketball tournament	Basketball tournament
Education	Nutrition assessment	Nutrition goal setting	Nutrition planning
Other	Fill in nutrition assessment form	Fill in nutrition goal-setting form	Plan a menu
Week 8			
Exercise	Continuous rhythmical exercise	Calisthenic super circuit	Continuous rhythmical exercise Sports and games
Education	Substance abuse pressure	Substance abuse prevention goals	Substance abuse avoidance planning
Other	Fill in pressure assessment	Group discussion	Role-play refusal skills
Week 9			
Exercise	Calisthenic super circuit	Continuous rhythmical circuit	Calisthenic super circuit Sports and games
Education	Violence prevention assessment	Violence prevention goal setting	Violence prevention planning
Other	Fill in assessment of violence in the neighborhood	Discuss goals	Role-play conflict resolution skills
Week 10			
Exercise	Fitness assessment	Continuous rhythmical exercise	Youths' choice
Education	None	Putting a program together	None
Other	Fill in fitness assessment	Compare scores to norms and set new goals	Award ceremony Discussion

Figure 10.2 *(continued)*

• **Planning.** A promotional plan helps create continuity and direction for all promotional efforts. Choose and present a consistent theme and message. For example, the consistent theme promoted by midnight basketball programs is playing by the rules. The message is to be off the streets at night participating in a constructive activity.

• **Contacting people.** Explore all avenues for disseminating promotional information. Contact people and gain their support for eliciting youth and others' involvement, such as participating youth and their friends, parents, community leaders, professionals such as educational and social service staff, and members of the media.

• **Varying promotional strategies.** Use a variety of promotional strategies for communication, meetings, and special events. The following are good examples.

Communication Strategies

- Newsletters
- In-house organizational communication
- Posters and flyers
- Written announcements
- Radio and TV announcements and interviews

Meeting Strategies

- Formal presentations to cooperating organizations
- Reports to local neighborhood councils
- Parent meetings

Special Events

- Kick-off events
- Tournaments such as state and inner city games
- Field trips
- Guest speakers
- Health fairs
- Family events

Unfortunately, many in the human service or education delivery area think that promotion is something that salespersons do. The challenge is to recognize that program promotion is an ongoing function that all must be involved in if the physical training program is to maintain support.

Facility Management Guidelines

Not all physical training programs have exercise facilities. Some organizations such as community recreation centers may have multipurpose facilities and probably have a facility management system in place. For others, the facility may be nothing more than a room where chairs are removed for an exercise class. Regardless of size, however, you need to address three areas for ensuring a safe facility: space configuration, equipment maintenance, and facility safety procedures.

• **Space configuration.** Configure the exercise space to allow separate space for flexibility and stretching, strength training, and cardiovascular endurance training. If you have room for exercise classes, make sure the class space allows at least 36 square feet per participant. If there is space for strength training equipment (free weights or machines), allow three feet between pieces of equipment.

• **Equipment maintenance schedule.** Set up a regular schedule for equipment maintenance, and install a monitoring system to document when maintenance is performed. Such a schedule might look like the following:

Daily Maintenance

- Wipe off equipment frames.
- Clean any upholstery with soap and water.
- Wipe off all seats and benches with soap and water.

Weekly Maintenance

- Inspect and adjust cables, nuts, bolts, and screws.
- Clean and lubricate any cables, chains, and pedals.
- Apply vinyl protectant to upholstery.

Monthly Maintenance

- Wash equipment grips with soap and water.
- Inspect equipment housing belts and electrical components.
- Calibrate equipment if required.

Biannual Maintenance

- Replace monitor batteries.
- Inspect for indications that equipment needs overhaul.

- **Facility safety procedures.** The following are some of the procedures to address if possible:
  - Ensure the facility meets all local fire safety codes.
  - Have signs in place covering the following areas: instructions for equipment use, rules of conduct for facility use, emergency procedures, and exits.
  - Assess the ventilation of the facility to see if the recommended 8 to 12 air exchanges per hour is met.
  - Assess the lighting to see if it meets the recommended 30 to 50 foot candles.
  - Assess heat and humidity to see if they meet the recommended guidelines to prevent heat stress (68 to 78 degrees and less than 60% humidity).
  - If possible, install flooring that is antistatic and nonabsorbent so it can be cleaned easily.

Record Keeping Guidelines

Program supervision and evaluation are seriously handicapped without good records. So maintaining accurate and up-to-date records of the physical training program is a necessity. The two major areas that require a record keeping system are youth information and program information records.

- Youth information records. Individual folders should contain all the information collected on participating youth such as the following:
  - Informed consent forms
  - Fitness program forms, such as fitness assessments
  - Attendance records
  - Written documentation of any behavior problem incidents
- Program information records. The standard information that should be recorded on a regular basis includes the following:
  - Program activities schedules
  - Total participant numbers, such as number of youth who have successfully completed the program
  - Records of unusual incidents, including participant injuries

Program Evaluation Guidelines

A serious problem for many community-based programs is that they are never evaluated. As a consequence, they tend not to be funded on a sustaining basis. Program evaluation is always required to ensure that a physical training program is being implemented effectively.

Having a well-designed and automatic program evaluation system in place not only helps document the effects of your program but also serves as a learning tool to show you how and where to improve your program. As program evaluation is a process of asking and answering questions, the goal of an evaluation design should be to answer two main questions: (1) How effective was the implementation of the program process? (2) How effective was the program in changing youths' fitness levels, risk factors, and problem behaviors? Address these two questions in process evaluation and outcome evaluation.

Process Evaluation. Process evaluation examines how the physical training program was delivered. The following are five questions those conducting a process evaluation should ask along with a strategy for answering each question.

1. What program activities and methods were provided by fitness instructors? Use a fitness instructor checklist to determine this.
2. Were all program activities delivered on schedule and in sequence? Again, use a fitness instructor checklist.
3. What program activities and methods appeared to be or not be of value? Survey fitness instructors, participants, parents, and the community.
4. What was the level of participation of youth assigned to the program? Keep attendance records.
5. What were the demographics of the youth served? Record demographics of participants.

Outcome Evaluation. Outcome evaluation seeks to discover if the program has accomplished its goals. Ask three questions, using the recommended strategy for answering each.

1. What changes occurred in fitness and activity levels? Collect youth questionnaire and fitness testing data before and after the program.
2. What changes occurred in risk factors (e.g., self-esteem, relationships, depression, anxiety) for problem behavior? Send out youth questionnaires and parent or community worker rating surveys before and after the program.
3. What changes occurred in problem behaviors, such as substance use patterns and violent or criminal behavior? Again, send out

youth questionnaires and parent or community worker rating surveys before and after the program.

Because of the nature of programming, it is not always possible to assess all youth on all measurements. You should, however, try to get as much youth data as is practical. A general guideline is to develop a yearly summary from the different sources of information to produce a formal program evaluation report that can be disseminated to organizational management or funding entities.

Supervision and Coordination Guidelines

In the planning section of this chapter, guidelines were listed for defining a functional organizational chain of command. A well-defined chain of command should make supervision and coordination somewhat automatic. The most important part of coordination is ensuring that operational tasks and functions are performed. The most important part of supervision is ensuring that staff are performing their respective coordination tasks and functions. Clearly defining position responsibilities for fitness leaders and supervisors greatly facilitates program supervision.

How much supervision is necessary? Daily monitoring and program supervision are the two levels of supervision. Daily monitoring is observing and overseeing both participating youth and staff. If everyone knows his responsibilities, this should not take much effort. Program supervision includes periodically reviewing program records and evaluation information and communicating regularly with youth, parents, and staff. Talking with those involved in the program provides immediate informal feedback on program operations.

When you have taken the time to clearly define all staff roles as well as organizational goals, the supervising is mostly monitoring, checking that the physical training program is accomplishing the program objectives.

Conclusion

Putting the physical training program together and coordinating it consistently requires as much effort as delivering the program directly to the youth. Leadership and programming (exercise, education, and related services) are the factors that directly determine the physical training program's effect. The coordination and administrative elements provide the integrating structure for those factors to interact smoothly. Moreover, addressing these organizational elements is vital because they provide program continuity and direction.

A Final Note

The focus of this book has been on the unique programming needs of at-risk youth. The rationale developed in part I explained those needs, and the guidelines for physical training programming and coordination presented in parts II and III were based on meeting those needs. The material has all been based on my experience, especially on successful applications of physical training programs.

The development and delivery of physical training programs with at-risk youth has been and continues to be a learning experience. One final principle I want to present is this: What works with at-risk youth is just as valid with all youth. Most youth have some deficits in life skills and values, but at-risk youth are extreme cases. They tend to have lower levels of life skills and have fewer parental and school control influences than other youth. Thus, their needs and the effects of programs are seen more clearly with this population. We can, however, successfully apply systematic physical training programs such as I have described to all our youth.

The final idea I would like to highlight is really an extension of what was presented in chapter 9 on leadership. It concerns the role modeling effect of the leader or instructor. In reflecting on the differences between physical training programs that are successful and those that are not, I have no question as to the major difference. Having an energetic, enthusiastic, and fit leader on the gym floor is the key, cutting across race, gender, age, and educational differences. "Walking the talk" is what it is all about. Anything less than that will not work—especially with at-risk youth.

Physical Fitness Test Procedures

This appendix consists of descriptions of the following physical fitness tests:

- Body composition with skinfold calipers
- One-minute push-up test
- Sit-and-reach test
- One-minute sit-up test
- One-mile run

Each description includes the purpose of the test, the equipment needed, the procedures, a script to use for instructing participants, and tips for administering the test. Before each test (except skinfold testing), read the script to the participants and demonstrate the test, pointing out common errors. Note that norms for all tests can be found on pages 97-98.

Skinfold Testing to Measure Percent Body Fat

Purpose. This method of assessment determines body composition by estimating percent body fat based on skinfold thickness measurements.
Equipment. Skinfold calipers and conversion chart. Measure in a private room that is at a comfortable temperature. You may wish to have a testing witness if you are measuring someone of the opposite sex.

Procedure

1. Identify the measurement sites. Use only the right side of the body unless some physical problem prevents it; in that case, use only the left side, and mark that fact on the records. The sites should include the following:

- **Triceps**—measure the vertical fold over the belly of the triceps halfway between the top of the shoulder and bottom of the elbow. Have the participant flex the elbow at a 90-degree angle.
- **Calf**—measure on the *inside* of the right leg at the level of the maximal calf girth. Have the participant place the right foot flat on an elevated surface with the knee flexed at a 90-degree angle. Grasp the vertical skinfold right above the level of the maximal girth and measure the skinfold at the maximal girth.

2. At each site, pinch from the top and measure from the bottom. Measure each site three times and record the reading for which you have two that are the same. If no two are consistent, move to the other site, measure it, then return to the first site and measure again.
3. Enter the site measurements, then add up the numbers from the two sites and use the chart.

   To use the chart in table A.1:
   - Find the correct gender form (boys or girls).
   - Find the column for the sum of skinfold measurements (Total MM) and locate the sum.
   - Look across to find the percent fat (% FAT). Record that number.

Tips for the Test Administrator

- When you pinch the skin, lift the skin and fat away from the muscle.
- When you pinch large, loose folds, ensure that you separate the skin and the fat from the connective tissue.

One-Minute Push-Up Test to Measure Upper Body Strength

Purpose. This test measures the muscular endurance of the upper body muscles in the shoulders, chest, and back of the upper arms (the extensors).

Equipment. Mat and stopwatch.

Procedure (Boys)

1. Have the youth place the hands about shoulder-width apart (see figure A.1). The fitness leader places a fist on the floor below the youth's chest.

Table A.1

FITNESSGRAM Body Composition Conversion Chart

BOYS*

Total MM	% FAT	Total MM	% FAT	Total MM	% FAT	Total MM	% FAT	Total MM	% FAT
1.0	1.7	16.0	12.8	31.0	23.8	46.0	34.8	61.0	45.8
1.5	2.1	16.5	13.1	31.5	24.2	46.5	35.2	61.5	46.2
2.0	2.5	17.0	13.5	32.0	24.5	47.0	35.5	62.0	46.6
2.5	2.8	17.5	13.9	32.5	24.9	47.5	35.9	62.5	46.9
3.0	3.2	18.0	14.2	33.0	25.3	48.0	36.3	63.0	47.3
3.5	3.6	18.5	14.6	33.5	25.6	48.5	36.6	63.5	47.7
4.0	3.9	19.0	15.0	34.0	26.0	49.0	37.0	64.0	48.0
4.5	4.3	19.5	15.3	34.5	26.4	49.5	37.4	64.5	48.4
5.0	4.7	20.0	15.7	35.0	26.7	50.0	37.8	65.0	48.8
5.5	5.0	20.5	16.1	35.5	27.1	50.5	38.1	65.5	49.1
6.0	5.4	21.0	16.4	36.0	27.5	51.0	38.5	66.0	49.5
6.5	5.8	21.5	16.8	36.5	27.8	51.5	38.9	66.5	49.9
7.0	6.1	22.0	17.2	37.0	28.2	52.0	39.2	67.0	50.2
7.5	6.5	22.5	17.5	37.5	28.6	52.5	39.6	67.5	50.6
8.0	6.9	23.0	17.9	38.0	28.9	53.0	40.0	68.0	51.0
8.5	7.2	23.5	18.3	38.5	29.3	53.5	40.3	68.5	51.3
9.0	7.6	24.0	18.6	39.0	29.7	54.0	40.7	69.0	51.7
9.5	8.0	24.5	19.0	39.5	30.0	54.5	41.1	69.5	52.1
10.0	8.4	25.0	19.4	40.0	30.4	55.0	41.4	70.0	52.5
10.5	8.7	25.5	19.7	40.5	30.8	55.5	41.8	70.5	52.8
11.0	9.1	26.0	20.1	41.0	31.1	56.0	42.2	71.0	53.2
11.5	9.5	26.5	20.5	41.5	31.5	56.5	42.5	71.5	53.6
12.0	9.8	27.0	20.8	42.0	31.9	57.0	42.9	72.0	53.9
12.5	10.2	27.5	21.2	42.5	32.2	57.5	43.3	72.5	54.3
13.0	10.6	28.0	21.6	43.0	32.6	58.0	43.6	73.0	54.7
13.5	10.9	28.5	21.9	43.5	33.0	58.5	44.0	73.5	55.0
14.0	11.3	29.0	22.3	44.0	33.3	59.0	44.4	74.0	55.4
14.5	11.7	29.5	22.7	44.5	33.7	59.5	44.7	74.5	55.8
15.0	12.0	30.0	23.1	45.0	34.1	60.0	45.1	75.0	56.1
15.5	12.4	30.5	23.4	45.5	34.4	60.5	45.5	75.5	56.5

(continued)

*Use the chart to determine percent body fat for all boys ages 5-16+.

Table A.1

FITNESSGRAM Body Composition
Conversion Chart (continued)

GIRLS*

Total MM	% FAT	Total MM	% FAT	Total MM	% FAT	Total MM	% FAT	Total MM	% FAT
1.0	5.7	16.0	14.9	31.0	24.0	46.0	33.2	61.0	42.3
1.5	6.0	16.5	15.2	31.5	24.3	46.5	33.5	61.5	42.6
2.0	6.3	17.0	15.5	32.0	24.6	47.0	33.8	62.0	42.9
2.5	6.6	17.5	15.8	32.5	24.9	47.5	34.1	62.5	43.2
3.0	6.9	18.0	16.1	33.0	25.2	48.0	34.4	63.0	43.5
3.5	7.2	18.5	16.4	33.5	25.5	48.5	34.7	63.5	43.8
4.0	7.5	19.0	16.7	34.0	25.8	49.0	35.0	64.0	44.1
4.5	7.8	19.5	17.0	34.5	26.1	49.5	35.3	64.5	44.4
5.0	8.2	20.0	17.3	35.0	26.5	50.0	35.6	65.0	44.8
5.5	8.5	20.5	17.6	35.5	26.8	50.5	35.9	65.5	45.1
6.0	8.8	21.0	17.9	36.0	27.1	51.0	36.2	66.0	45.4
6.5	9.1	21.5	18.2	36.5	27.4	51.5	36.5	66.5	45.7
7.0	9.4	22.0	18.5	37.0	27.7	52.0	36.8	67.0	46.0
7.5	9.7	22.5	18.8	37.5	28.0	52.5	37.1	67.5	46.3
8.0	10.0	23.0	19.1	38.0	28.3	53.0	37.4	68.0	46.6
8.5	10.3	23.5	19.4	38.5	28.6	53.5	37.7	68.5	46.9
9.0	10.6	24.0	19.7	39.0	28.9	54.0	38.0	69.0	47.2
9.5	10.9	24.5	20.0	39.5	29.2	54.5	38.3	69.5	47.5
10.0	11.2	25.0	20.4	40.0	29.5	55.0	38.7	70.0	47.8
10.5	11.5	25.5	20.7	40.5	29.8	55.5	39.0	70.5	48.1
11.0	11.8	26.0	21.0	41.0	30.1	56.0	39.3	71.0	48.4
11.5	12.1	26.5	21.3	41.5	30.4	56.5	39.6	71.5	48.7
12.0	12.4	27.0	21.6	42.0	30.7	57.0	39.9	72.0	49.0
12.5	12.7	27.5	21.9	42.5	31.0	57.5	40.2	72.5	49.3
13.0	13.0	28.0	22.2	43.0	31.3	58.0	40.5	73.0	49.6
13.5	13.3	28.5	22.5	43.5	31.6	58.5	40.8	73.5	49.9
14.0	13.6	29.0	22.8	44.0	31.9	59.0	41.1	74.0	50.2
14.5	13.9	29.5	23.1	44.5	32.2	59.5	41.4	74.5	50.5
15.0	14.3	30.0	23.4	45.0	32.6	60.0	41.7	75.0	50.9
15.5	14.6	30.5	23.7	45.5	32.9	60.5	42.0	75.5	51.2

*Use the chart to determine percent body fat for all girls ages 5-16+.

Reprinted, by permission, from *The Prudential FITNESSGRAM reporting procedures for non-computer users,* 1992 (Dallas: The Cooper Institute for Aerobics Research).

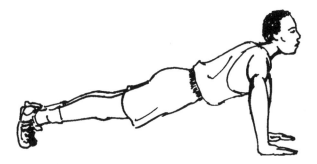

Figure A.1 One-minute push-up test (starting position).

2. Starting from the up position with elbows fully extended, have the youth lower the body until the upper arms are parallel to the floor and the chest is touching the leader's fist. Then have the youth push up again. Ensure that the youth keeps the back straight, and in each extension up, locks the elbows. Allow resting in the up position.

3. The score is the number of push-ups completed correctly in one minute.

Procedure (Modified Push-Up for Girls)

1. Have the youth begin in the starting push-up position as shown in figure A.1 with elbows fully extended and back straight, but have her place the knees on the floor with lower legs and feet tilting up (see figure A.2).

Figure A.2 One-minute modified push-up test (starting position).

2. As the fitness leader, get in position to observe the chest touching the floor.

3. Have the youth lower herself until her chest touches the floor, then have her push up again. The youth can rest in the up position.

4. Again, the score is the number of push-ups completed correctly in one minute.

Script

Use the following script to prepare the participants.

The push-up measures the muscular endurance of the upper body (chest, shoulders, and triceps). Place your hands on the ground wherever they are comfortable, approximately shoulder-width apart. Your feet may be together, or up to 12 inches apart. Your body should be in a straight line from the shoulders to the ankles, and must remain that way throughout the exercise. When I say "Go," lower your body by bending your elbows until your upper arms are parallel to the ground. I will tell you when you have gone low enough. Then return to the starting position by straightening your arms. You may rest in the up position. Do as many correct push-ups as you can in one minute. Your score will be the number of correct repetitions you do. Watch this demonstration . . . . Are there any questions?

Tips for the Test Administrator

- Ensure that male participants maintain a relatively straight line from their shoulders to their ankles.

- Be alert for "head bobbers," that is, participants who move their heads up and down without lowering or raising their bodies.

- Position yourself at a 45-degree angle to the participant's head and shoulders. From there you can see if the participant lowers the body until the upper arm is parallel to the ground as well as check for correct body alignment.

- Youth who wear glasses should remove them for this event if they do not have a retaining band.

Sit-and-Reach Test for Flexibility

Purpose. This test measures the flexibility of the lower back and upper leg area (hamstrings).

Equipment. Sit-and-reach box: a 12-inch–high box with a yardstick attached to the top, the 9-inch mark at the edge, and the 36-inch mark pointing away from the participant.

Procedure

1. Have the participant warm up slowly by practicing the test.
2. Have the participant take off the shoes and sit on the floor, legs extended at right angles to the box. Have the participant touch the near edge of the box with the heels, which should be eight inches apart. Make sure that the yardstick is centered above the person's legs (see figure A.3).

Figure A.3 Sit-and-reach test.

3. Have the participant slowly reach forward with both hands (one on top of the other) as far as possible and hold the position for one second. (Do not allow the participant to bounce, as this could harm the low back.) Have the participant reach three times.
4. Record only the farthest reach, to the nearest 1/4 inch.

Script

Use the following script to prepare the participants.

The sit-and-reach test measures the flexibility of your low back and hamstrings. After you warm up, take off your shoes and sit with your legs flat on the floor and heels against the box, about eight inches apart. Place one hand over the other, bend forward at the waist, and reach as far forward as you can. Don't bounce. Exhale as you gradually lean forward until you can't reach any farther. Hold that position for one second. You will have three tries at this event, with your best effort counting as your score. Watch this demonstration . . . . Are there any questions?

Tips for the Test Administrator

- Monitor participants to ensure that they lean forward gradually and don't bounce.
- Make sure participants keep their legs flat on the floor.

One-Minute Sit-Up Test
to Measure Abdominal Strength

Purpose. This test measures the muscular endurance of the abdominal muscles.

Equipment. Mat and stopwatch.

Procedure

1. Have the person lie on the back with knees bent and heels flat on the floor. Hands should be crossed over the chest (see figure A.4). Have a partner hold down the feet.

Figure A.4 One-minute sit-up test.

2. Have the person perform as many correct sit-ups as possible in one minute. In the up position, make sure the individual touches the elbows to the thighs, then returns to a full lying position before starting the next sit-up. They can rest in the up position.
3. The score is the number of correct sit-ups performed in one minute.

Script

Use the following script to prepare the participants.

> The sit-up measures the muscular endurance of the abdominal muscles. Lie on your back with your knees bent at a 90-degree angle and your heels on the mat. Your feet may be together or apart, but the heels must stay in contact with the mat or ground. Your partner can hold them for you but can't kneel on them. Your hands must stay crossed over your chest throughout the test. When I say "Go," curl your upper body by bending at the waist. Touch your elbows to your thighs and return to the starting position. When returning to the starting position, your shoulders must touch the mat. Your partner will count a repetition each time you return to the starting position. Do not arch your back or lift your buttocks off the mat. If you fail to keep your hands on your chest or touch your shoulders to the mat, or if you arch your back or lift your buttocks, you will receive a warning. After one warning, such a repetition doesn't count. You will have one minute to do as many sit-ups as possible. I will give signals at the last 45, 30, and 15 seconds, and will count down the last 10 seconds. Your score is the number of correct sit-ups you do in the minute. Watch this demonstration . . . . Are there any questions?

Tips for the Test Administrator

- Make sure that the arms remain crossed over the chest.
- Make sure that the knees remain at a 90-degree angle throughout the exercise.
- Make sure that the buttocks stay in contact with the floor at all times.
- Note that resting in the up position is allowed.

One-Mile Run to Test for Cardiovascular Endurance

Purpose. This run is a measure of cardiovascular endurance, or aerobic power.

Equipment. A 440-yard track or marked, level course; a stopwatch.

Procedure

1. Have participants warm up and stretch before the run.
2. Have participants line up at the starting line. Instruct them to cover the distance as fast as possible. Give the command "Go" and begin timing. If several participants run at once, call out their individual times at the finish and record them later. It helps to have an assistant to record scores.

3. Have participants cool down after running the course by walking for an additional five minutes or so. This prevents venous pooling, a condition in which the blood pools in the lower extremities so less is returned to the heart, possibly leading to dizziness or fainting. Walking enhances the return of the blood to the heart, which assists with recovery.

4. The score is the time it takes to run the course to the nearest second.

Script

Use the following script to prepare the participants.

> The one-mile run measures your cardiovascular endurance and the endurance of your leg muscles. You must complete the run without any help. At the start, you will line up behind the starting line. When I say "Go," the clock will start. You will begin running at your own pace. To complete the mile, you will need to run [tell the runners how many laps they must run, or describe the course, including the finish line, if not run on a track]. Your goal is to finish the mile in as fast a time as you can. You may walk, but walking will increase your time. I will call off your time at the end of each lap [if running on a track] and will record your time later. Are there any questions?

Tips for the Test Administrator

- If you run the test on a track, instruct the participants to move out of the inside lane if they decide to walk.
- Using an assistant test administrator will give you flexibility in case someone needs help during the event. The assistant can either take over timing duties or provide help to the participant. Otherwise, you may lose control of the event.
- If running in two groups, assign partners. Ensure that each pair of partners has a pen or pencil, and encourage one to write down the finish time as soon as the other one finishes.
- If running in one group, have the runners call off their names and the lap being completed each time they cross the start-finish line. Keep track of the laps completed on a list of the participants' names. If you have one or more assistant test administrators, divide the names among them.
- The timer should call off the times in minutes and seconds as the runners approach the finish line.

Adapted, by permission, from T.R. Collingwood, R. Hoffman, and P. Sammann, 1995, *FitForce Coordinator Manual* (Champaign, IL: Human Kinetics), 183-197.

Index

Note: Page numbers referring to figures or tables are followed by an "f" or a "t," respectively.

About the Author

Thomas R. Collingwood has delivered and installed more than 100 physical fitness programs for at-risk youth—from suburban school youth to inner-city youth to incarcerated juvenile offenders. He developed and instituted the First Choice fitness program as a substance abuse and violence prevention intervention for at-risk youth. The program was cited as one of 20 exemplary youth fitness programs at the National Youth Fitness Summit. It was also selected by the American College of Sports Medicine (ACSM) as one of four youth fitness programs recommended for further application nationwide to meet the Public Health Service's Healthy People 2000 goals.

Collingwood developed and directed the Dallas Police Department's Youth Services Diversion Program, which reduced the rearrest rate for program youth from 50 percent to 10 percent. Started in 1974, the program was named the Outstanding Diversion Program in the State of Texas and is still in operation today. He also developed and directed the continuing education program for the Cooper Institute for Aerobics Research, a program that has trained more than 20,000 fitness leaders worldwide.

Collingwood has served as a YMCA director and has authored more than 100 publications in the field of physical fitness. He is a recipient of the Healthy American Fitness Leader award, presented annually by the President's Council on Physical Fitness and Sports and the National JAYCEES to recognize the top 10 fitness leaders in the United States.

A fellow of the ACSM and the American Psychological Assocation, Collingwood earned his PhD in psychology from the State University of New York at Buffalo. He is president and director of his own business, Fitness Intervention Technologies. He and his wife, Gretchen, live in Richardson, Texas.

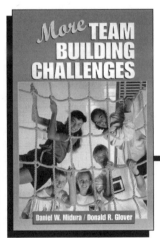